Republicans on the Potomac

Books by John Franklin Carter

Mystery:

Murder in the State Department
Murder in the Embassy
The Corpse on the White House Lawn
Scandal in the Chancery
Slow Death at Geneva
The Brain Trust Murders
Death in the Senate

Fiction:

The Rat Race
Champagne Charley
Hangover Hall (*in preparation*)

History and Politics:

Man Is War
Conquest: America's Painless Imperialism
The New Dealers (*in collaboration*)
American Messiahs (*in collaboration*)
Our Lords and Masters (*in collaboration*)
What This Country Needs
What We Are About to Receive
LaGuardia: A Biography
The Future Is Ours
1940
Remaking America
The Catoctin Conversation

Autobiography:

The Rectory Family

REPUBLICANS ON THE POTOMAC

The New Republicans in Action

BY JAY FRANKLIN

WILDSIDE PRESS

To S.S.C.

"THE best political community is formed by citizens of the middle class. Those states are likely to be well administered in which the middle class is large, and larger if possible than both the other classes, or at any rate than either singly; for the addition of the middle class turns the scale and prevents either of the extremes from being dominant."

Aristotle, *Politics*

CONTENTS

FOREWORD

TWENTY years ago, in collaboration with Ernest K. Lindley, I wrote *The New Dealers*, a sympathetic but non-partisan appraisal of the personalities and policies of the first administration of Franklin D. Roosevelt. Subsequently, for many years, I supported those policies in my writings, in government service, and in politics.

It is never easy to break the political associations of a lifetime, but I have found it possible to work with those whom I helped to defeat in 1948 and still retain the friendship of many of the honorable Democrats with whom I fought shoulder to shoulder in the past for bitterly contested reforms which are now taken for granted. The more I saw of the progressive Republicans of the East and the Far West, the more I believed that these were the kind of Americans to whom the country must turn for leadership if we were to avoid national disaster.

Many of the figures in the Eisenhower administration are my personal friends, as are many of the Democrats whom they have displaced. As I see it, our two-party system is really a reciprocal undertaking in which both sides agree on so many issues that their points of differ-

11

ence serve to create political progress without major dislocation of our public life. There is a vast area of good will and common agreement in American government which is the heritage of the party in power, be it Republican or Democrat. The chief purpose of the system is, therefore, to provide a simple practical means to change the directing personnel and the emphasis of public policy without national upheaval.

So far as was possible under a rigid time schedule, I have tried to make this appraisal of the New Republican movement thorough and accurate. I wish to express my thanks to the busy officials of the Eisenhower administration for the time and trouble they have generously taken to advise me in this work.

This is, of course, an expression of my own opinions and judgment on public men and events. The responsibility is entirely my own and, while I have gone to pains to assure historical and factual accuracy, the interpretation is wholly personal to myself. If I have succeeded in making it clear that the New Republicans are the true heirs and honest executors of the reforms the progressives and liberals helped to pioneer a generation ago, then I shall feel that I have kept faith with all those in both parties who have worked through the years to make America and the world a better place.

JAY FRANKLIN

Albany, N.Y.
April 2, 1953.

Republicans on the Potomac

I

LOCAL BOY MAKES GOOD

1. The Republican Resurrection

DWIGHT D. EISENHOWER is not the leader of the New Republican Party which has taken over the Federal Government after twenty years of Democratic control; he is not the agent of that group of able, ambitious younger men and women who engineered the nomination and election of the first professional soldier to be chosen President in eighty years. Instead, he is the expression of the deep historical process which has resurrected the Republican Party and has made it a new political movement, just as Franklin D. Roosevelt's New Deal transformed the old Democratic Party into a new, semi-revolutionary movement. Together, he and the New Republicans have brought their new party to office under an overwhelming mandate to deal wisely and effectively with the greatest national crisis in American history.

President Eisenhower would be the first to agree with this estimate of his relation to political events. For the

15

New Republicans are both a product of and a reaction to the same forces which sent a farm boy from Abilene, Kansas, to walk with kings and lead nations in arms. They are not "the rich, the wise, and the good" whom Alexander Hamilton exalted as our destined leaders; neither are they the Republican bankers and industrialists and railway magnates who developed the continent and alternately enriched and impoverished the nation for three generations after the Civil War.

Their leaders are not men like Mark Hanna or Boies Penrose or either of the Roosevelts. Few of them were born to any recognizable degree of wealth or had the initial advantages of assured social position or the privilege of an expensive education. Most of them come from small towns, many of them from west of the Mississippi River, and all of them have succeeded in their own careers by the traditional process of free competition. They are the kind of Americans who work their way through college and make their own opportunities; incidentally, the majority of them are of the old American stock with roots far back in Colonial America.

They include Republican governors who taught the old elephant new tricks during the long period of Democratic centralization of the national government. They include representatives of industrial and financial managements which survived and prospered in the face of economic depression and labor unrest. They represent the middle-class professional and business groups which resent the cycle of inflation and war into which liberal Democratic leadership has plunged the nation in the last fifty years. What is perhaps the most important fact about the New Republicans is that they have survived and come to power by learning to think and act as a team. Eisenhower is not their master.

The Democratic Party, which they have displaced, has always tended to follow the "star system," to rally its forces around a powerful, dramatic personality: a Thomas Jefferson, an Andrew Jackson, a William Jennings Bryan, a Woodrow Wilson, or a Franklin Roosevelt; colorful, dramatic personalities, with great gifts of political leadership, men whose principles and ideals have made history—and casualty lists. To tell the truth, the Democratic Party is still beglamored by the Napoleonic vision which established their party, the miracle of a single man of genius reshaping nations and institutions by the blend of personal ambition, political imagination, and military force.

Where the Federalist ancestors of the Republican Party were merchants and landowners in the tradition of the eighteenth-century British Whigs, the Democrats combined the monarchical instinct of the Tories with the rise of the common man. Since the days of Julius Caesar, this process has always led to political violence. Where Theodore Roosevelt enrolled the cowboys and the dudes in his famous Roughriders, his Democratic cousin Franklin combined the professors and the labor leaders in his New Deal political machine, while under President Truman the alliance between the New Deal millionaires and mobsters threatened to corrupt and destroy representative government in the United States.

The weakness of a party which depends on a powerful and fascinating personality for its existence is that it cannot be sure that a supply of such personalities will always be available for the Presidency. The strength of the contrasting team approach to political action—which is also essentially the military approach—is that no member of the team is indispensable, that there are reserves to draw on while the struggle continues, and that the members of the team look to each other rather than to any single player for success.

That is why President Eisenhower fits the New Republican Party as a glove fits the hand. He is the American Dream, walking. He is "Local Boy Makes Good." He represents the slow, steady, selective processes of personal ability, individual character, and outstanding achievement in fair, open competition. His is not the Horatio Alger story of "rags to riches." Neither is the Eisenhower story like the legend of Ulysses S. Grant, a drunken failure, rusting in quiet desperation until summoned to play a great part in history by the trumpet call of great events.

This is a different kind of story. It is the tale of old stock, solid Americans in every part of a large country, working and living and trying to do their duty to their nation and their family and their God. It is the America of Currier & Ives which has marched on Washington, the small towns where girls in pigtails play hopscotch and learn to cook and go to Sunday school, where small boys whoop and scuffle in the piles of autumn leaves around the Soldiers Monument, and neighbors need not lock their doors at night. It is the America which for generations has been educating its boys and girls and sending them out into the world to make a living, the America which pays its debts and goes to church and volunteers in time of war. It is the salt of the American earth, the essence of our society, the hope of our future, the very best we have.

Whether our very best will be good enough to deal with the tremendous crisis confronting our people remains to be seen. There are other dreams struggling for expression in Eisenhower's America. There is the dream of perpetual and increasingly workless material abundance, through science, socialism, taxes, and bureaucracy, which has fascinated our people since the turn of the century. There are vestiges of the old, ugly vision of a society based on privilege—of color, race, faith, or wealth. There is the new nightmare of a Marxist world, dedicated to the permanent revolution and the economic thrust toward mass management of politics and police-imposed social solutions. And there is the strong missionary faith that one hundred and sixty million Americans are in some way destined to direct humanity and redeem the world from evils and customs which have existed since the dawn of human history.

Out of these conflicting dreams arose the New Deal of 1932, with its vision of social justice and its simple faith that no American problem existed which could not be set right by the simple applications of good will, human reason, and abundant Federal appropriations. But the final expression of these alluring concepts proved to be painfully old. Called upon to devise better ways to distribute the fantastic industrial and agricultural abundance of a fantastically wealthy continent, the only solution offered was to redistribute insecurity, to ration opportunity, to destroy or give away wealth, and to impoverish everybody by monetary inflation. Called upon to find employment for the ten million Americans thrown out of work by depression and technology, the only solution was to put them in uniform and send them into armed combat in a great war which our own abundance financed and won. Called upon to protect and promote the security of the American people and the world-order in which they had grown to nationhood, they threw away the military victory our soldiers had won and exposed the nation to a far worse danger than the one we had fought and conquered in the greatest war in history.

So with Eisenhower and the New Republicans the American people have gone back to first principles, to character rather than personal charm, to wisdom rather than intellectual ingenuity, to the very sources of our national strength.

This is not characteristic of our history. In previous times we have been restless, optimistic, impatient of the past, convinced that "history is bunk" and that all human ills can be cured by swallowing some magic dose—sewing machines, tractors, television sets, nationally advertised brands of cigarettes, coffee, or chewing gum. We have believed that penicillin was better for us than sassafras tea, that forty miles an hour was better than twenty miles an hour, and that three hundred and fifty miles an hour was better yet. Now we find ourselves, against our plans and desires, in a world which has always been dangerous for fools and which today punishes stupidity far more promptly and severely than ever before.

Hence Eisenhower and the New Republicans in Washington and hence the drama of the American people's decision to send their best team onto the field in what may mean the very life or death of western civilization. The issues are so much vaster than those which Roosevelt confronted cheerfully in 1933 that they outstrip imagination and almost numb public opinion. All of the problems of the gallant New Deal enterprise twenty years ago were subject to domestic legislation. But President Eisenhower and his party cannot legislate for Russia, for China, for Western Europe, or the British Commonwealth. Mere human intelligence will not dispel the danger. What we need now are patience, wisdom, fortitude, endurance, sacrifice. We have turned to the national reservoir of these ancient virtues. It is on them that our safety and survival now depend.

2. WHERE "IKE" FITS IN

If Eisenhower had not existed it would have been necessary to invent him.

In one sense, America did invent him, since a nation's capacity to solve its problems is measured by its unplanned ability to create the kind of men and women it needs to serve it. The forces which developed Eisenhower lay deep in the story of the whole American people. And those forces decreed that a man like "Ike" should be born in the right part of the country, at the right time, of the right kind of parents, and that he should marry the proper wife and follow the right career to bring his abilities to full maturity at the time when they were most needed.

Back in the 1880's, when that erudite Scot, James Bryce, whom Theodore Roosevelt once described as an enormous brain entirely surrounded by whiskers, wrote *The American Commonwealth*, he was not unduly discouraged by the greed, crudity, and corruption of American society and politics. He announced that the regeneration of America lay in the class of idealistic, college-bred Americans of good family who resembled those cultured Englishmen whose high ideals and integrity were willing to lose half the Empire and wreck half the globe rather than yield to tyrannical world-conquest.

If another Bryce had been studying us in the first decade of the twentieth century, he would have been compelled as a true prophet to lift his eyes from Boston's Back Bay, from Hyde Park and Oyster Bay, and from Princeton (where a young Virginian named Tommy Wilson was already in Bryce's time a promising student of history and government). To foretell the aftermath of that deluge of nineteenth-century good intentions and twentieth-century bad administration, he would have had to look to places which no respectable English or American scholar had ever heard of: to Peru, Nebraska; to Cheboygan and Owosso, Michigan; to Minerva, Ohio; to Yerba Linda, California; to Killeen, Texas, and East Dover, Vermont; and above all to Abilene, Kansas.

For the New Republican Party was to find its leadership in the small country towns of America, particularly in the Middle West and on the Prairies which have served as the nation's granary for nearly a hundred years.

It was in this granary that Eisenhower was born. The year was 1890, when Benjamin Harrison was President and what were later called "the good old days" were raging throughout a nation without a single automobile.

Raging is the word. The 1890's were a time of trouble for the American people and the storm-center of those troubles lay in Kansas, which was determined to "raise less corn and more hell" in protest over low grain prices and high living costs. That was the period of the Haymarket murders in Chicago, the bloody Pullman strike, the panic of 1893, the Populists, and Bryan's campaign for "Free Silver"—a period of angry upheaval against the periodic miscalculations and mishaps of a haphazard financial system, a period which witnessed the ominous growth of socialist and syndicalist ideas among the foreign-born masses still crowding into the eastern cities. No small boy living in Kansas in this period could have escaped the passions and enthusiasms of the age. The same prairies which produced Bryan, the matchless voice of social justice in his day and age, also produced William Allen White, an equally sensitive social observer, whose famous editorial "What's the Matter With Kansas?" helped to calm the storm which swept the prairies in that feverish decade before William McKinley's "Full Dinner Pail," the discovery of Klondike gold, and the Spanish-American War ushered the young western republic into world affairs.

At the time, the war with Spain seemed very gay and thrilling, except perhaps to those who died of yellow fever or wounds, but it meant that, before the Abilene youngster finished grade school, a fateful national decision had been taken, a decision which was ultimately to bring him to the White House as President of the United States. For Teddy Roosevelt charging up San Juan Hill and Admiral Dewey sinking the Spanish warships in

Manila Bay were the first steps in a march which was to lead to Chateau-Thierry and the Argonne, to Monte Cassino and the Bulge, to Tokyo Bay and Yalta and Potsdam. Young America had sat down at the poker table and bought a small stack of chips in a game which has always been played for table stakes, with stacked cards, brass knuckles, and knockout drops.

While Eisenhower was still in high school, Great Britain had sensed the need for allies in her coming struggle with the German Empire. The whole nature of war and politics was changing. Barbed wire and the machine gun, like the submarine and airplane, were part of the tremendous scientific forces which destroyed four empires in four years and could destroy civilization and the human race. As a consequence, this catastrophe insured that, after half a century of peace, prosperity, and progress, the American people would again need good military leaders. It also meant that eventually, as with Washington and Grant, a military career would become a prerequisite, rather than a disqualification, for the Presidency of the United States.

3. "Ike" and Mamie

Tell me how you spent the first ten years of your life and I will tell you what kind of a man you are. Show me the woman you married and I will tell you where you are going. On both accounts, Eisenhower commands respect.

He was born in Denison, Texas, on October 14th, 1890, the son of parents of old Pennsylvania Dutch stock whose ancestors had come to this country from Germany two generations before the American Revolution. In 1878 his grandfather emigrated to Abilene, a Kansas frontier town, with a group of the River Brethren, one of the Pennsylvania Dutch sects, similar to the Amish and Dunkards.

"Ike's" father, on coming of age, rejected the life of a farmer, opened a general store in Abilene, and failed. After this misfortune, he moved to Texas where David Dwight Eisenhower (later changed to Dwight David and then to "Ike," first a family and then a West Point nickname) appeared as the third of seven sons, all but one of whom are still living. Two years later the family returned to Abilene, where the father of the future President got a job as night watchman and mechanic in the creamery operated by the Brethren and where his mother struggled with the problem of raising seven boys on the earnings of a husband who never made more than a hundred and fifty dollars a month in all his life.

What this meant to young Dwight David was a boyhood spent in a hardworking, hard-up, happy, God-fearing home. He wore hand-me-down clothes to the public school, worked on farms during vacation, and finally landed a job as "second engineer" or fireman in the local creamery, where he worked a seven-day, eighty-four-hour week at low pay. That was when he was nineteen years old; it is small wonder that his thoughts turned to the army or the navy as a more stimulating career. His mother encouraged him, although she was personally a pacifist and later was to become a Jehovah's Witness. With the help of the local editor, he made contact with Kansas's progressive Republican Senator Bristow, and went to Topeka to take the examinations for both West Point and Annapolis in the spring of 1911. He passed first for the navy and second for the army and, but for being over the age for admission to Annapolis, might well have become an admiral. The age hurdle swung him over to West Point and he was enrolled as a cadet the following autumn in the last hush before the onset of the first World War.

His record at the Point was fairly good. He was especially adept in English and history, played some football until he received a knee injury which almost kept him out of the army, and graduated 61st in a class of 168 on June 12th, 1915. At that time a whole generation of generals and statesmen were learning, at the expense of the "poor bloody infantry," that barbed wire and the machine gun had entirely changed the art of war. The *Lusitania* had been sunk, but America was still neutral and "Ike" went into the infantry as a matter of course. He was assigned to Fort Sam Houston in Texas as a second lieutenant.

There he met and promptly fell in love with a young lady from Denver, Colorado who was spending the winter in Houston. She was Mamie Geneva Doud, a pretty, dark-haired nineteen-year-old Iowa girl whose father had been a successful Chicago meat packer before moving to Colorado in 1902. The couple were married in Denver on July 1st, 1916 on the same day that Eisenhower received his promotion as first lieutenant.

Slender, vivacious, and loyal, Mamie Eisenhower was a preordained army wife, prepared for a life of sudden moves, long absences, no settled home, and continuous anxiety. The army became her life, her husband's career became her masterpiece. They had two children. Their first son, named for his father, was born in 1917, after we had entered the first World War, and was to die of scarlet fever the year Warren Gamaliel Harding became President. This was the greatest personal tragedy in Eisenhower's life. The second son, now Major John Sheldon Doud Eisenhower, was born in Denver in the summer of 1922 and graduated from West Point the very day his father launched the D-Day attack on fortress Europe on June 6th, 1944.

The future first lady was not only a preordained army wife; she was also a preordained Republican wife, who believed and practiced the ancient principle that a woman's place is with her husband and family. She stayed in the background and worked for her husband's interests, accepting without complaint the abrupt shifts and changes of an army career.

As a matter of fact, one of the questions now agitating

"social" Washington is whether Mrs. Eisenhower shall be allowed to maintain her political detachment. She is certainly not an ardent partisan politician like Mrs. Roosevelt, neither has she served as her husband's political secretary and adviser like Mrs. Truman. Not since Grace Coolidge has there been anyone remotely resembling her in the White House. And she has already proved that she is a great asset to her husband's political career.

The man in the crowd in a small North Carolina town who yelled, "Gee, Mamie! You even look good in a dressing gown!" when she and "Ike" turned out of their Pullman berths on a frosty morning, spoke for millions. She has learned to dress extremely well, that is to say, suitably to herself and in good taste, rather than expensively. Her "surrey with the fringe on top" hair-do has not only affected feminine fashions; it suits her own personality and facial contours.

At the age of fifty-six, with streaks of gray in her brown hair, she is unaffectedly pretty, lively and, true to her prairie tradition and her partly Swedish ancestry, is an excellent cook, with special preferences for corn on the cob, fried chicken, home-baked beans, and cornbread. And she fits perfectly into the general picture of the old yeoman Americans taking over the government of their country, in that her father's people emigrated from England to Connecticut in 1639, while her mother's father, Carl Carlson, came from Sweden to Iowa in

1868. It scarcely seems probable that as first lady she will be allowed to confine herself to her favorite hobby of interior decorating—that was done to the White House, and how! by the Trumans—or be satisfied with purely family affairs. After all, Ike's career is still her life work and here she can and does contribute much.

At the outset, "Ike's" career was not very promising. He never saw overseas service in the first World War. In fact, when he led the North African invasion, he had had no combat experience and had never seen a battle. However, he had already demonstrated his remarkable ability as a trainer of soldiers, combining imagination, discipline, and leadership to a degree that kept the army's eye on him for future reference. In the 1920's he was shifted from army post to army post, graduated first in his class at the Command and General Staff School at Fort Leavenworth, and was generally liked and trusted by his fellow-officers. But the most important assignment he drew in that period was eight months in France with the United States Battle Monuments Commission. He was, in short, a perfect specimen of the average regular army major in peacetime, serving out his time with no particular prospect of promotion before the age of retirement.

During that period an army career offered few chances to the average line officer. But whatever assignment he received he did thoroughly and well. Just as he had uncomplainingly accepted training-camp duty in the first World War, so he undertook to do some "ghost writing" in the War Department after his return from his battle monuments assignment in France. He made himself useful in drafting speeches for Hoover's Assistant Secretary of War Payne. When Douglas MacArthur became Army Chief of Staff, that eminent connoisseur of a resonant prose style latched onto "Ike" and later took him along as his own chief of staff when he was transferred to the Philippines in 1935. "Ike" remained with MacArthur in Manila until January of 1940, when World War II had already begun to pose a major military problem for the United States and we were about to engage in the first peacetime conscription law in our history.

His abilities, seasoned by work in organizing the Philippines Constabulary, now found fuller scope. As chief of staff for General Kreuger, he distinguished himself by "defeating" Ben Lear's army in the great Louisiana maneuvers of 1941. Army Chief of Staff George C. Marshall promptly collared "Ike" for work in the War Plans (Pacific Theater) Division of the War Department. He did so well in this job that, somewhat irrelevantly, he was slated for the North African command. When the North African invasion was in the making, he disagreed significantly with Marshall on where the landings should take place. From a purely military angle, "Ike" argued that the landing should be well inside the Straits of Gibraltar. Marshall was uncertain of Spain's political attitude and decided that one landing should also be made at Casablanca on the Atlantic coast of French Morocco. Marshall's view naturally prevailed; the incident is worth reporting because it showed that at that time "Ike" had a blind spot for the political factor in military operations.

This blind spot came to the fore again, with far more serious effect, when he was in command of the European invasion. Winston Churchill, political to the tip of his cigar, was already concerned over the Soviet advance. Churchill wanted to invade the Balkans and push on to Berlin, and threatened to "lay down the mantle of my high office"—Winstonian for "to resign"—if "Ike" insisted on the invasion of Southern France in Operation Anvil. Churchill objected that this would strip the Mediterranean theater of a mobile land force which could be used in the Balkans as a counterpoise to the Red army. "Ike" had his way in this and other political matters and some of the present Berlin entanglement is undoubtedly due to his decision to fight his part of the war on strictly non-political lines.

Other examples of this political astigmatism are suggested by his apparent approval of the army's "point system" for repatriating our troops from Europe after V-E Day and by his reported responsibility for abandoning the elaborate military government program the army had prepared for the occupation of Germany. The "point system" automatically stripped our European forces of experienced cadres and thus advertised to the Russians our assumed intention to withdraw entirely from Western Europe. The failure in military government led to graft, black marketing, and scandal in Occupied Germany. It was not until the appointment of former Assistant Secretary of War John J. McCloy as United States High Commissioner that the mess was finally cleaned up.

Yet it is fair to say that Eisenhower's capacity to learn from mistakes is a valuable part of his military outlook. He was given the European command because Marshall respected his brilliance as a strategist and also because he had shown that he could get on with people. When he returned to Europe in 1951 as supreme commander for NATO, he was astutely conscious of, and skilled in dealing with, the political factors of his multi-national command. Indeed, his wartime experience had already trained him in the delicate arts of personal diplomacy in handling such diverse personalities as George Patton, Charles de Gaulle, Omar Bradley, and Field Marshal Montgomery.

Victory in Europe found Eisenhower at a pinnacle of military reputation, a five-star general with lifetime rank and pay. He returned to Washington as Chief of Staff in 1945, setting Marshall free to go into Chinese politics under Truman's fatal directive. During the three years of his tour of duty, "Ike" traveled extensively in Canada, Japan, China, Korea, Mexico, Panama, Brazil, and Europe. He had already visited and toured Russia after the V-E Day triumphs. He knows the world, or at least he knows a world—the world of armies and statesmen—better than any other American in history. Then, when Omar Bradley was about to take over as Chief of Staff in 1948, Ike was offered and accepted the presidency of Columbia University and retired from active service.

At the time, the job looked like the American equivalent of the dukedom with which Britain rewarded the famous Marlborough who had humbled the armies of Louis XIV two hundred and fifty years ago. Nobody had thought of Eisenhower as an educator, although his army record showed that he was a first-class instructor, and it is probably true that few people do so think of him. He served less than two years in a position which would tax the experience of a professional academic administrator, did a superb job for Columbia, and also found time to advise the Joint Chiefs of Staff regularly through this period.

Then, in December of 1950, President Truman recalled Eisenhower to active service to organize NATO's defense of Western Europe. So, early in 1951, the general returned to France and, except for some quick trips home in order to report on his assignment, there he remained until June of 1952, when his name had been so prominently mentioned politically that he found it inconsistent to remain on military assignment.

The man who had refused to forestall the Russians in seizing Berlin and who had brushed aside Churchill's political advice was now acclaimed as the free world's leader in the crisis provoked by the failure of British and American politicians to foresee the political consequences of their own victory. European opinion cooled so rapidly toward Eisenhower's candidacy after the Democrats nominated Governor Stevenson that it is quite probable that European commitments under NATO were partly designed to prevent the nomination of a Republican isolationist for the Presidency. With the defeat of the Taft forces at Chicago, the Europeans made no secret of their preference for continuing a Democratic administration at Washington. This apparent ungraciousness toward the man who had previously led them to victory was chiefly due to the natural human instinct to avoid any change. The Europeans were not sure that they wanted a more positive national policy on the part of the American government. They knew where they stood with Truman and Acheson; with Eisenhower they were far from sure.

For after twenty years of American presidents and secretaries of state who had been highly co-operative, they could not know whether the New Republicans would continue the same policies and maintain the same unquestioning compliance with London, Rome, and Paris as in the past. By the time of Eisenhower's election by an earthquake vote on November 4th, there was no longer any doubt that his political victory was highly unpalatable to the very governments which had previously hailed him as the tireless and tactful organizer of the defense of western civilization against the Soviet empire and its Communist dogmas.

4. "IKE's" POLITICAL EDUCATION

At the age of sixty-two, tall, well set-up, with sandy hair receding from a capacious forehead and sharp blue eyes, President Eisenhower can flatter himself on the swiftest political education *summa cum laude* in the history of the Republic.

It is the fact that he has learned so fast which has disturbed the chancelleries of Western Europe. Eisenhower is the same general who in 1945 was so naïvely unprofessional as to hate the Nazi officers whom he fought. He is the same general who, as recently as 1949, hesitated to endorse the senatorial candidacy of his friend John Foster Dulles lest he modify his own political standing. He is the same general who in the winter of 1951–52 approved a statement by the manager of his affairs that if the Republican Party wanted him they knew where to find him, although no man has ever had the Presidency thrust upon him.

However, his carefully prepared homecoming speech at Abilene, Kansas was a political anti-climax and was saved from flat failure only by "Ike's" obvious sincerity of purpose. While his lieutenants were sweating and toiling down in the hot steamy plains, fighting to win him the nomination, he remained cool in the high altitudes of Denver, fishing, painting water colors, and uttering what would have sounded like schoolbook platitudes except for the fact that he obviously meant them. Yet, even then he was actively making political contacts and his train trip to Chicago was a masterful piece of intensive campaigning.

Even after he had come to Chicago and accepted the nomination as a call to duty, as the start of a crusade— an echo, perhaps, of his book *Crusade in Europe*—his did not begin until September. The conduct of his Denver headquarters was lame and undistinguished. By the end of August even his best friends were frankly dismayed and Roy Howard, the friendly publisher of the New York *World-Telegram*, said publicly that he was "running like a dry creek." Then came the legendary "Battle of Morningside Heights," in which it was made to appear that "Ike" had capitulated to the conservative wing of the Republican Party as personified by his beaten convention rival, Senator Taft. This led Senator Wayne Morse to run screaming from the Republican Party in the direction of the Democratic candidate, who used the alleged surrender to Taft as an issue in his own campaign.

Next came the Nixon affair, when the Republican nominee for the Vice-Presidency was represented as having been the recipient of improper financial favors in California. Nixon managed to clear up his position to the general satisfaction of the Republican part of the public but it was a close call and it burned some of the dew off the Republican rose.

Yet there was massive wisdom and masterful strategy behind these disturbing appearances. The South was wooed and partly won; most of the Taft Republicans buried their disappointment and worked for "Ike's" victory; and, most important of all, the Democrats fell into a mood of overconfidence, as bland and as blind as that which had cost the Republicans the election of 1948. History had served them, then, to show that the party in power at a time of general prosperity cannot fail to win a national election. They did not believe it would ever happen.

In the last ten days of the campaign, "Ike" suddenly closed the gap between himself and the despondent progressive Republicans of the East and the Far West in a crushing pincers movement which transformed what might have been only a narrow Republican victory into a landslide. It was a tidal-wave election, which swept Eisenhower into the Presidency with a huge plurality of electoral and popular votes and which also insured Republican control of both branches of Congress. It was also notable that, as the campaign came to its smashing conclusion, "Ike" had finally mastered the art of speaking to people, in huge crowds as well as in small intimate groups.

This was Eisenhower's personal achievement, for he ran far ahead of his party's other candidates, especially in the Middle West where the reverse had been feared. This achievement stemmed from the fact that political generalship, like military generalship, depends chiefly on the imponderables.

To begin with, "Ike" is a man of steady habits; hard-working, energetic, an early riser, with the calm nerves and good digestion which history finds most useful to a military commander. He does not worry, he works regular hours, he eats sensibly, takes a drink in the evening, goes to bed and sleeps soundly, and is up early again ready to work the following day.

"Ike" is much more versatile than this steady routine would suggest. He is a fair singer and has been known to give a good parlor rendition of "Drink to Me Only with Thine Eyes." Mrs. Perle Mesta, former American Minister to Luxembourg, reports that Eisenhower, on a visit to her legation, insisted on being turned loose in the kitchen, where he prepared and baked an excellent lemon meringue pie, all with his own big hands. Like Winston Churchill, he is an amateur painter, but where Churchill's work is obviously that of a gifted amateur, "Ike's"— notably his portrait of the great golfer "Bobby" Jones —is of high professional quality and suggests the close portrait technique of John Sargent rather than the impressionism of George Bellows. He obviously enjoys fishing, but apparently more for the relaxation than for the catch. He is also an enthusiastic golfer, playing a very good game, and likes to win.

He is also a deeply and articulately religious man. Brought up in the country of the camp meeting, the revivalists, the Holy Rollers, and the regular Thursday evening prayer meeting, he feels no self-consciousness at invoking the blessing of God when his cabinet assembles or in opening his inaugural address with a public prayer. A good many Americans feel a slight sense of personal embarrassment at such public invocations of the Almighty, but in "Ike's" case there is no doubt that he sincerely believes in the power of prayer and is humble enough in spirit to pray without Rooseveltian self-righteousness.

Another important element in his character is his incredible charm, His smile is gay and infectious, even when the blue eyes above it remain cool and appraising. His skill in handling Congressional committees was proverbial in the War Department and he has the general reputation of being able to charm the birds off the bough. It is on record that he talked the French out of Dakar in 1941, where the British had met with fierce resistance a year earlier. Despite his numerous tiffs with General Montgomery, he became firm friends with the peppery little British military genius. He is actually able to appear diffident and disarming even in matters on which he is expert. He makes you want to help him accomplish what he desires. Women in particular are attracted by his personal magnetism and one of the phenomena of his campaign was the repeated spectacle of teen-age girls and older women jumping up and down with excitement at his public appearances.

Yet when all is said and done with charm, it remains a fact that most of all Eisenhower commands respect, inside and outside the army, inside and out of politics. He is a strong, full-blooded, able man of his own age and generation. He has tremendous self-control and rarely loses his temper; when he does it is a field day. He has performed every task given him with skill, competence, and a marked economy of time and effort. He knows the world and has seen more of it, physically, than any American chief executive. And he remains essentially what he began as: one of a large, hard-up, hard-working, God-fearing happy prairie family, who was expected to make his own way in the world, honestly and responsibly, and to do his duty uncomplainingly at all times.

These are admirable qualities in any man: in a President they represent a national dividend on the spirit and institutions of the people who developed them and on the part of the country from which he came.

Stating it another way, Eisenhower represents the best we have in character, experience, and ability. His is the thankless and difficult task of leading the nation and the free world through the greatest crisis since the fall of Constantinople to the Turks five hundred years ago this very year. Whether our best will be good enough remains to be seen, but that question need not arise because, if it fails, the whole of American history, western civilization, and Christianity itself become meaningless.

The final key to Eisenhower's administration is supplied by his choice of the word "crusade" to describe his purpose. He has come forward, quite simply, to remind us that duty, service, and sacrifice are the price of human freedom, and he is prepared to ask of others what he himself has given: a single-hearted devotion to the public good. In this he is perhaps the first modern American leader to envision a higher purpose in government than the materialism which has shaken down empires like ripe fruit in his own lifetime. Of him it could truthfully be predicted, "If war is too important to be entrusted to the generals, peace is too precious to be committed to the politicians." As a professional soldier, he has seen the waste and suffering of war. The world may yet take comfort in the knowledge that none of the professional soldiers who have served as President of the United States has ever involved this country in a war. It is only the civilians who are bellicose. Soldiers prefer peace and can bring to its service the same moral standards of responsibility which they are expected to bring to war.

II

KINGMAKERS

1. A PRESIDENT

EVERY man and every woman who worked for Eisenhower's nomination and election is a political kingmaker. Even the comparatively small group of American citizens who actively directed his victory in 1952 must include scores of names entitled to honorable mention in the annals of the New Republican Party. A few men can be selected arbitrarily as representatives of the much larger group which constituted the high command of the Eisenhower movement. Some who opposed him helped him by their very opposition. High on the list of those responsible for his presence in the White House were two generals, two minister's sons, the son of the publisher of a small Midwestern newspaper, and a bankrupt haberdasher who had been brought up on a hard luck farm in western Missouri.

These last two represented Franklin Roosevelt's two great political mistakes. Roosevelt never forgave himself for allowing Governor Lehman to name Thomas E.

43

Dewey his special prosecutor of rackets in 1935 and thus providing the young man from Owosso, Michigan with a springboard which tossed him into the Governorship of New York State and twice made him the Republican Presidential candidate. And Roosevelt never realized the miscalculation he had made in selecting Harry S. Truman as his Vice-President in 1944, because apparently it did not enter the wartime President's head that he might not serve out his full term and that a man of far less experience and much less breadth would handle the peace settlement after World War II.

Former President Truman must receive a large share of the real credit for Eisenhower's election. The cantankerous, courageous, erratic, and thoroughly human little sexagenarian from Kansas City was the first public man on record to favor Eisenhower as his successor.

Now is not the time or the place to judge Mr. Truman as a political leader. The power of the Presidency is a prism which breaks up a man's character into its constituent elements, revealing the defects and limitations, as well as the virtues, of the chief executive, all terribly magnified. Minor qualities which would be condoned or even unnoticed in ordinary life thus become facts of tremendous significance in national and even world affairs. Very few men in our history—possibly only George Washington and Abraham Lincoln—still shine as steadily after their political leadership as they did before power beat upon them. Before he was through with General Eisenhower, Truman had boxed the compass of political conduct and had contributed powerfully both to his election and to the success of his administration.

The first point to be noted in this strange association is Mr. Truman's attitude toward military men. An able artillery captain in the first World War, he positively adored successful generals. One of his close associates in the 1948 campaign said: "If Harry Truman had been a woman, he would have been a camp follower." Truman regarded General George Marshall as the greatest living American and, when he met Eisenhower at the Potsdam Conference in July of 1945, he told the leader of the crusade in Europe that he—Truman—would help "Ike" get anything he wanted, including the Presidency.

Mr. Truman soon regretted this unsolicited offer when the Americans for Democratic Action and other prominent Democratic Party leaders made no secret of their desire that General Eisenhower rather than Truman should be their Presidential candidate in 1948. However, Eisenhower set his mind at rest by withdrawing his name from consideration and Truman went ahead and received the nomination, winning the election in a photo finish against Governor Dewey.

Two years later, however, President Truman returned to the idea that Eisenhower would be "available" for the Democratic nomination and recalled him to military duty as commander of the NATO forces for the defense of western Europe. This post constituted a world-wide showcase and it does not seem to have occurred to Truman to discover whether the general was a Republican or a Democrat. Even if he had any doubt on this point, he seems to have believed that the offer of the Presidency was one which would induce Eisenhower to change his affiliation on terms which would allow him to win by acclamation. It was only late in 1951, as reported by Arthur Krock of the New York *Times*, that Truman took the trouble to check up and received the dismaying news that, if Eisenhower ran for the Presidency, it would be as a Republican.

It was then that Mr. Truman made his final contribution to the general's political triumph. He informed former Senator Burton K. Wheeler of Montana that "Ike's" place in history was so assured and respected that he would never consent to have his name and reputation dragged into the mud of politics. Then, when this estimate of the general proved to be a profound miscalculation, Mr. Truman proceeded to supply the vituperation needed to confirm an Eisenhower landslide. He implied that "Ike" was a racial bigot, he accused him of "demagoguery" in promising to go to Korea, he "declassified" secret documents in an attempt to prove that "Ike" was responsible for the Korean entanglement, he went around the country denouncing the idea of electing a military man to a position which had become one of tremendous military responsibility. The crowds chuckled and cheered and whooped, "Pour it on, Harry!" and the

Democratic President believed he was winning the election for his own party.

He only succeeded in diverting public attention from the real Democratic Presidential candidate, Governor Adlai E. Stevenson of Illinois, and thus converted a fairly close campaign into a Republican landslide. When the votes were counted, not one man in the White House had anticipated the outcome. It was, perhaps, the greatest miscalculation in the life of any American politician in our times.

It was then that President Truman made his most valuable contribution to American public life. This testy, arrogant little bantam of a machine politician was at times capable of a queer humility. He had been awed and humbled when Roosevelt's death pitchforked him into the White House. He had been modest and unassuming when, much to his own surprise, he won the election of 1948, though his entourage soon got him over that passing mood. In the moment of final humiliation and defeat, after one last snarl, the outgoing President offered the full co-operation of his discredited Democratic administration in turning the Federal Government over to the victorious Republicans, smoothly, in good temper, and with a strong sense of public responsibility. Whatever place history may assign to Harry S. Truman, it can truthfully be said that naught became his administration like his leaving of it. Despite occasional outbursts of verbal backsliding, he thus did honorable service to the nation.

History records that Franklin D. Roosevelt refused the proffered co-operation of the Hoover administration in 1932. Twenty years later, both Eisenhower and Truman made political history by setting a precedent for real co-operation in the interregnum period between the defeat of one party and the accession to power of its opponent.

In his case, this was not so difficult as it seemed twenty years earlier. Both Truman and Eisenhower came from the same neck of the woods. Both had been born of poor, hard-working families. Both had a simple, strong, unquestioning American patriotism. Both were religious-minded men, Truman a Baptist and "Ike" a Presbyterian. Both had been in battle and both represented that middle-income American group which made up the bone and sinew of the Republican Party.

The differences between them were those of temperament, experience, and formal political affiliation. Truman was a professional, lifelong machine politician; Eisenhower a professional, lifelong soldier. Truman was excitable, Eisenhower calm. Truman was as unreliable as a slippery plank, Eisenhower was as steady as a rock. Truman's intimates played him like an accordion, Eisenhower led his associates like the captain of a ball team. Truman was a Democrat who happened to be the leader of a Democratic Party which had been in power for twenty years. Eisenhower had only recently and reluctantly entered political life as a Republican, from a sense of duty to his country in the crisis provoked by the policies of those twenty Democratic years. But they were more united by those qualities which they shared than they were divided by their differences of character and outlook; together they set an example of forbearance and good feeling which can be listed among the enduring assets of the first Republican to be elected President of the United States in a generation.

2. A GOVERNOR

Of all the Republicans who planned and worked for Eisenhower's victory, New York's Governor Thomas E. Dewey made the outstanding contribution. Paradoxically and characteristically, he made it by subordinating his own personality to the creation of a winning Eisenhower team.

Other governors worked with Dewey during the months which preceded the Republican 1952 Convention. John Lodge of Connecticut, Sherman Adams of New Hampshire, Albert Driscoll of New Jersey, Payne of Maine, and Inglis of Washington were prominent among them. But the three-times-elected Governor of the state which contains a tenth of our population and pays a fifth of our taxes, the man who was twice nominated for the Presidency and had overcome the crushing political disappointment of defeat without complaint or bitterness, had more to offer than any other of "Ike's" political supporters.

Alert, neat, scrappy, Dewey at the age of fifty had learned how to elect and keep in power a Republican administration in a state which had been strongly Democratic for twenty years. He had shown that he could be a good loser as well as a graceful winner. His was, possibly, the finest political brain in American politics and his interests and acquaintances were world-wide. A chess player rather than a poker player, he repeatedly infuriated the experts by his quiet habit of making successful combinations in Republican politics. Yet the Eisenhower movement was built, politically, on Dewey's character quite as much as on Dewey's skill in party management and public appeal.

That character had been systematically misrepresented by his opponents both inside and outside the Republican Party. Resolute, he was called ruthless; warm hearted, considerate, and even diffident by nature, they said he was cold-blooded and arrogant. Deeply loyal to his friends and associates and sincerely religious—he is a vestryman of St. Paul's Episcopal Church at Albany—the smear artists of both parties portrayed him as cruelly ambitious, a machine boss with complete and arbitrary control of party organization. Even his zeal as a public prosecutor in convicting murderous racketeers was twisted to suggest that he took a sadistic pleasure in sending men to prison.

In addition to all this, some Republicans went so far as to hold him personally responsible for not being elected

President in 1948 and his various moves in the long, difficult battle to win Eisenhower the Republican nomination were greeted with bitter anger by the advocates of other candidates.

Through all this period, Dewey kept his head and his temper. He played clean, hard politics. He had already shown his moral stature by not brooding over the failure of his Presidential candidacies, where men as big as Al Smith and Jim Farley had visibly sulked for years, while even Herbert Hoover nursed a long grievance over his defeat in 1932, as his published memoirs make clear.

In 1950, Dewey had thought to retire from public life in order to practice law, educate his two sons, and live on his dairy farm in Pawling, New York. He was not permitted to do so and, after a strong and, as usual, highly successful campaign, was re-elected Governor of New York for the third time. The following summer, at the suggestion of John Foster Dulles, he took a journey to the lands of the Far Pacific and returned in time to place his experience and knowledge at the service of the Eisenhower movement. It is the best tribute to his character that he found far more pleasure in working for "Ike's" nomination and election than he ever had in any of his own political campaigns.

Dewey, like Eisenhower, came from the great Midwestern region of America; his parents, like "Ike's," were of old Colonial stock. His original American ancestor, Thomas Dewey, came to Boston in 1630. Tom Dewey was born on March 24th, 1902 over a general store in Owosso, Michigan, a town of about eight thousand people, where his father, a former West Point cadet, edited the local Owosso *Times*. He grew up in the pleasant ways of the Booth Tarkington type of midland small town—selling *The Saturday Evening Post*, handling the local distribution of the Detroit *News*, working on farms or in the local drugstore during school vacations, playing football, debating, playing in minstrel shows at high school, and doing all the pleasant things young Americans did in those easy days before the first World War. He also worked as a printer's devil in his father's printing shop and during the summer vacation of his junior year at college he actually ran the shop and edited the paper.

His family was far from wealthy and he put himself through his first year at the University of Michigan on money he had earned for this purpose. He studied singing and, in his last year before his graduation in 1923, won first prize in a state singing contest. He then won a scholarship with a New York voice teacher at the Chicago Musical College where he met a young mezzo-soprano from Oklahoma named Frances Eileen Hutt, whose father was a brakeman on the Union Pacific. After she had returned to New York, he came east, continued his singing lessons, and also enrolled in Columbia Law School. He still has a fine baritone voice but he gave up a singing career after a minor throat operation reminded him of the risks of a professional vocalist. That was in

1925—mid-stream in the era of wonderful nonsense—but Tom Dewey had his law degree and settled down in September to practice law as a junior clerk at eighteen hundred dollars a year. Three years later, when his salary had climbed to three thousand dollars, he decided it was enough to marry on and he did. His bride was the same Frances Hutt he had met in Chicago.

This tale has been told before, but it is a good story and it is worth telling again, if only because it provides the key to the much larger political pattern of his and Eisenhower's career. It is a story of decency, ability, fidelity, tenacity—the story of a couple of ambitious young people coming to the metropolis to make a living and to found a family rather than to pursue a career.

While a middle-aged army major named Eisenhower was still working with the Battle Monuments Commission in France, a young lawyer named Dewey was enrolled in the New York Tenth Assembly District Republican organization and was doing the humdrum political chores of ringing door bells and watching the polls in a Tammany stronghold, unaware that in 1931 he would suddenly find his foot on the bottom rung of the great political ladder and start climbing.

Dewey has never stopped except for brief rests since that day when the newly appointed Republican United States Attorney for the Southern Judicial District of New York, George S. Medalie, asked him to serve as his chief assistant; at twenty-nine, he was the youngest man ever to hold that post.

The rest of the Dewey story is a matter of public record. He ran Medalie's staff of sixty lawyers successfully, prosecuting every kind of case, including the famous case against racketeer "Waxey" Gordon. After Medalie's resignation, the nine Federal judges appointed Dewey as United States Attorney until F.D.R. replaced him with a regular Democrat. Eighteen months later, by mid-1935, a disgusted New York County Grand Jury was demanding a special prosecutor to investigate New York City's rackets. Lehman resisted for two months, then finally gave in and named four eminent members of the bar under instructions to agree on which of them should take the assignment. At the end of their conferences, they announced that thirty-three-year-old Dewey was the man, and Lehman grudgingly appointed him. He ran the rackets investigation for two and a half years and then in 1937 ran for and was elected as district attorney in New York, winning by over a hundred thousand in the worst defeat Tammany ever suffered. In May of 1938, Dewey indicted, and later convicted, Tammany leader "Jimmy" Hines in a body blow at the Democratic combination of crime and politics in New York. That same year, he was nominated for governor by the Republicans and most politicians believe he was actually elected, being "counted out" by sixty-four thousand votes in his race against the incumbent Herbert Lehman who was supported by all the other parties, including the Communists.

Dewey was a candidate for the Republican Presidential nomination in 1940, but was edged out quite easily by the Wendell Willkie steamroller. At the end of his term as district attorney in 1941, he declined renomination and returned to private practice. A year later he was elected governor with a whopping majority and was re-elected in 1946 and in 1950, each time with heavy pluralities.

In 1944, he accepted the thankless but necessary job of running for the Presidency against F.D.R., then at the height of his war popularity. Four years later, after a sharp tussle with Senator Taft of Ohio, he was again nominated for the Presidency and would have been elected but for an overconfidence among Dewey's supporters which enabled Truman, who had the benefit of the ablest political advice in America, to drift in as the winner of the closest national election in this century.

Two years later, faced with an incipient cabal in New York State Republican politics, the governor reluctantly put aside his personal preference for private life and allowed himself to be drafted for the governorship, and by definition for a major role in the 1952 campaign. For this third victory left him in an unassailable position to contribute to the success of his party, by virtue of the fact that it was at last clear to everyone that he was not motivated by personal ambition and was ready to give "Ike" the best he had.

What Dewey had was tremendous.

He produced the team-play principle, as opposed to the Democratic Party's preference for prima donnas, whether it was F.D.R. trying to play every instrument in the band or Truman rendering "The Missouri Waltz." He had long since shown that he was one of the few men in public life who would not take "Yes" for an answer. He was still rarer in his refusal to take "No" for an answer either, until he had heard the reasons. This kind of leadership wins football games, political campaigns, and wars. It provided "Ike" with the bridge from SHAPE to GOP.

Dewey also contributed the Dewey program, a "We *can* do it better!" record in Albany which showed how an honest Republican administration which believed in social progress could deliver the goods, simply, economically, and without bureaucracy or regimentation. The Dewey program had also proved that it could win majority support, year after year, in a normally Democratic state. Even if "Ike," in the broad simplicities of prairie Republicanism, didn't appreciate its importance, here Dewey gave him the political key to 1956 and 1960. Possibly that was what "Ike" had in mind when, shortly before his inauguration, he referred to Dewey as a man whose political future still lay before him. The governor would disagree emphatically, but the Washington commentators, those professional exporters of educated guesses, decided that this meant Dewey as President some time soon.

He contributed the technique of television campaigning which he had invented in 1950, a method so effective it could not be omitted and so expensive that it delighted advertising agencies and gave gray hairs to campaign-fund raisers.

Finally, Dewey supplied Eisenhower with the most practical kind of help. The Dewey team was sent into action. Herbert Brownell, Dewey's long-time political partner and campaign manager, was brought into action to manage "Ike's" pre-convention campaign. Republican State Chairman Pfeiffer, a hard-headed Buffalo lawyer, was set to work helping round up Eisenhower delegates. Sardonic Irish-born Tom Stephens, Republican State Secretary, was turned loose in the primaries, first in New Hampshire, then in crucial New Jersey. Jim Hagerty, the governor's press secretary, was assigned to work with Brownell three weeks before and at the Chicago Convention and subsequently became "Ike's" campaign press representative; Gabriel Hauge, the young Minnesota economist who has since been installed in the White House, was recruited from *Business Week* to help "Ike" on economics. Dr. Stanley High was ripped from *The Reader's Digest* to help "Ike" on speeches. Batten, Barton, Durstine & Osborn—the famous New York advertising firm which had been Dewey's ally for a decade—rolled over to the general's support on September 15th, after "Ike's" radio and television had been mismanaged. A special research unit, headed by Dewey's Commissioner of Commerce, Harold Keller, and including Dewey's Mediation Chairman, Mervyn Pitzele, and Hickman Powell of the State Power Authority, also was sent into action.

His help included himself, and week by week, despite the pangs of literary parturition involved in the production of his first book, *Journey to the Far Pacific*, and the legislative session at Albany, the governor sat in on the conferences, advised, planned, and directed, until the moment came for the most eloquent speech he delivered in the entire 1952 campaign. That speech was delivered at the Chicago National Convention of the Republican Party. It was brief; it was unanswerable. Amid a chorus of howls and boos from galleries allegedly packed by the Chicago *Tribune*, Dewey made this oration: "New York casts ninety-one votes for General Eisenhower, four votes for Senator Taft." This was a mild preview of the 848,000 majority Dewey's state was to give the general in November.

In summary, it can safely be said that, although Eisenhower finally won the election almost by national acclamation, he would not have been nominated at all without the self-effacing, astute, and disinterested support of Governor Thomas E. Dewey.

3. A SENATOR

Senator James Henderson Duff of Pennsylvania was second only to Governor Dewey in achieving the nomination and election of President Eisenhower.

Like so many in the New Republican movement, Duff is a Presbyterian. In fact, he is the son of a Presbyterian minister, of that pugnacious Scotch-Irish blood which gave Pittsburgh politics so much dash and color. It is typical of the political atmosphere of that smoky town that former Democratic Senator Joe Guffey, who used to be a business friend of Duff's, remarked in 1950: "Jim Duff has been a good Governor of Pennsylvania and he will be a good United States Senator. Of course, we haven't spoken for years since he called me a Communist."

Seventy years old, six feet tall, weighing about two hundred pounds, with blue eyes and crew-cut red-gray hair, the junior Senator from Pennsylvania made his way up from the rectory at Mansfield (now Carnegie) in Allegheny County, through the rough-and-tumble of oil and gas leases into the bare-knuckle free-for-all that distinguishes the politics of that region. He was a successful "wildcatter" in the oil and gas business—as later in public life—which he entered by the somewhat obscure route of graduating from Princeton in 1904 and studying law at the University of Pennsylvania and later at Pittsburgh University. He was a promising athlete at Princeton, although never 'varsity material, and his younger brother Joe, who was killed in World War I, was an all-American football star.

Jim Duff first tried his hand at politics with Teddy Roosevelt's Bull Moose campaign in 1912 and after that fiasco returned to the regular Republican fold with a hearty suspicion of the Old Guard. However, his plans for making a fresh political career were postponed in 1929 when he, along with a good many other Americans, went broke. He was still paying off his debts, with an occasional free-swinging romp in the Republican state organization, when Governor Martin drafted him for state attorney general in 1943, when Duff was already sixty years of age. Four years later Duff ran for the governorship, was elected, and then broke sulphurously with Joe Grundy's Old Guard Republican machine in eastern Pennsylvania. From that day to this, Duff's simple test of political affiliation is whether a man is for or against Joe Grundy and the Old Guard Republicans in the Keystone State.

By that test, he opposed Dewey at the 1948 Republican Convention. By that test, he smashed the Old Guard in the 1950 primary which resulted in sending Duff to the Senate and Judge John S. Fine to the governor's mansion at Harrisburg. By that test, he lined up against Taft and Grundy in 1952, helped "Ike" win the Pennsylvania Presidential primary with over eight hundred thousand votes, and completed his task, after a bitter feud with Governor Fine, by swinging forty-four of Pennsylvania's seventy convention votes to Eisenhower and helping bring Pennsylvania into the Republican column on election day with a majority of over a quarter of a million votes.

He was a good progressive Governor of Pennsylvania during his four-year term, putting a stop to stream-pollution and compelling strip mines to replace the top soil on their cuttings. He managed the state's finances prudently, despite a great hospital- and road-building program, and he became nationally famous when he ordered highway commission bulldozers to spill the parked trucks over the side of the Pennsylvania Turnpike after the truckers staged a sit-down strike on the roadway in protest against paying suitable tolls. When he entered the Senate in 1951, everyone expected more fireworks from "Big Red."

They were disappointed. The new senator devoted his first two years in Washington to promoting the candidacy of General Eisenhower. One of the first moves in this game was a general treaty of amity and commerce with Governor Dewey. The two men had so much in common that their quarrel of '48 was forgotten and, starting late in 1951, Duff and Dewey conferred in New York on the average of once a week, planning "Ike's" pre-convention strategy. These New York meetings were secret affairs at the Commodore Hotel and usually included Herbert Brownell, Tom Stephens, New York National Committeeman Russel Sprague, and later

Henry Cabot Lodge of Massachusetts and Senator Frank Carlson of Kansas.

Two incidents indicate how delicately balanced were the personalities which decided the success of their campaign. For some weeks, Herbert Brownell hesitated to give full time to the Eisenhower campaign on the sound ground that he had committed himself to his firm not to become involved in another political campaign. This aroused unfounded suspicion in the Duff camp that Dewey might secretly consider himself the eventual candidate, and in the spring Dewey finally persuaded Brownell to devote his full time. Again, when Duff went down to Texas, had a brisk quarrel with Henry Zweifel, the Taft leader, and struck up a warm friendship with Jack Porter, later leader of the Eisenhower forces in the Lone Star State, the Dewey group were alarmed and took Duff to task for preferring a fight to victory. Later Brownell went to Texas and moved in to capitalize dramatically on the failure of the Taft forces to deal fairly with the elected Eisenhower delegates at the Mineral Springs Convention. Paradoxically, the Taftite grab of the thirty-six Texas delegates, which was denounced as "theft" by the "Ike-likers," ended with the latter getting all the Texas delegates, including eight who fairly belonged to Senator Taft.

Duff's style of campaigning is simple and neolithic. Dewey stayed close to New York City and did his major campaigning via television. By election day, the governor had actually appeared on television more than any other political leader except Governor Stevenson. But Duff went everywhere and spoke everywhere. Before the votes were counted he had traveled over one hundred thousand miles and had delivered hundreds of speeches in support of the general.

But the victory was won before the campaign began, in the course of those quiet, regular New York meetings in which Dewey and Duff forged that mutual trust and understanding of their aims and methods which created the moral atmosphere for the Republican triumph. It is no easy thing for strong, able men to agree in politics, particularly when one of them is Duff and the other Dewey, each of whom has vigorous personal convictions and a willingness to go to bat for them at any time and in any place.

With Brownell as the competent political chief of staff, the man who got things done, and with Cabot Lodge neglecting his own political fortunes to act as traveling salesman for Eisenhower, the Dewey-Duff combination proved irresistible. It paid off in enough delegates to nominate the general on the first ballot and in enough votes on election day to make Eisenhower the first Republican President with a broad popular mandate in twenty-four years.

As a matter of record, Duff was *almost* the first national Republican to come out for Eisenhower. That was in 1948, when it was believed that Duff's support of

"Ike" was intended chiefly as a move to stop Dewey. The latter was actually the first national Republican leader to come out for Eisenhower: he spoke for "Ike's" nomination as early as October of 1950 and stuck to his position, whereas Duff, despite his detestation of the Old Guard, voted for Taft in 1948.

The Old Guard angle is vitally important, for a large part of the significance of the Eisenhower movement derives from the fact that its original leaders were chiefly eastern Progressive Republicans. They were men who had fought Old Guard Republican machines, and sponsored and administered liberal social programs as governors of such industrial states as New York, Pennsylvania, and New Jersey. They were also men who had broken with their party's traditional isolationism in order to advocate aid to Europe and such other controversial measures as universal military training, which had been forced on the American people by the challenge of the "cold war" with Soviet Russia.

Men like Duff and Dewey and Driscoll were branded as "Me-too-ers" by their Old Guard opponents, but they had pointed the Republican way back to national power by refusing to allow the reactionaries to dominate public policy. Such men had also discovered, what President Eisenhower will swiftly learn, that in a pinch an honest Republican executive can always count on decent Democratic votes, in the legislature or at the polls, to carry the day for progressive government against the reactionaries in the ranks of both parties.

Still happily married after nearly forty-five years to the bride of his youth, Senator Duff stands high among the kingmakers of the Eisenhower administration. He is also a living reminder that the New Republicans are considerably older than the Republic. His own ancestors came to New England in the early 1630's and his later forebears settled in western Pennsylvania six years before the American Revolution. The old Scotch-Irish breed is tough and Jim Duff is tough. He represents an America which, he believes from the soles of his firmly planted feet to the tips of his bristling reddish hair, is morally and physically tough, decent, and self-respecting.

4. A Publisher

Many able editors and many powerful publications, including such giants of journalism as the New York *Times* and the New York *Herald-Tribune*, as well as men like Roy Howard and the Cowles brothers, campaigned vigorously for General Eisenhower.

But none of them made as effective a contribution to "Ike's" crusade as did Henry Robinson Luce, co-founder and directing genius of the most successful publishing venture of the twentieth century, the *Time-Life-Fortune* magazine empire.

That is because Luce contributed to "Ike's" cause not

only favorable editorial treatment but also personnel. Luce lent two of his editorial aces, C. D. Jackson and Emmet Hughes, as campaign speech-writers after "Ike's" opening utterances had showed the need of fewer platitudes and more punch lines in the oratorical contest against the adroit and witty Adlai Stevenson. Luce also encouraged his wife, the talented Clare Boothe Luce, to campaign tirelessly for the general and made the significant negative contribution of not supporting Robert A. Taft. This he might well have done since Luce and Taft were fellow-members of Yale's legendary Skull-and-Bones Society and were also linked by close ties of friendship with Taft's personal campaign manager, Dave Ingalls of Cleveland.

Harry Luce is a remarkable man.

He is the son of a missionary in China. Harry was born in Tengchow, China in 1898, on the eve of the Boxer Rebellion, and spent his boyhood in the Far East. Presbyterian missionaries don't usually have much money to finance a college education for their children, but Harry was sent to Hotchkiss School, to prepare for Yale, under the patronage of Standard Oil's Mrs. Edward Harkness. That was in 1912, the year of Republican division and downfall. Harry entered Yale in 1916 and graduated with the class of 1920, having taken time out to serve as second lieutenant of field artillery in the first World War.

As an undergraduate, Luce was fiercely eager to succeed. A friend of Thornton Wilder and Steve Benét, he wrote poetry. He also wrote for the Yale *Daily News*, where he and another Hotchkiss boy, Briton Hadden, made plans for a weekly news magazine. On graduation, he staked himself to a year at Oxford and then returned to get direct newspaper experience on the Baltimore *News*, where Hadden was already working as a reporter. In the winter and spring of 1922, he and Hadden made detailed plans for the publication which eventually appeared in the spring of 1923 as *Time, the Weekly Newsmagazine*.

The first seven years were the hardest and the publication did not show a profit until 1928, but it taught Luce the secret of success. He paid high salaries and gave stock to his associates. Since he picked able editors and trusted them, this method worked magnificently. In 1930, he started *Fortune*, a de luxe job of business reporting edited by the left-wing poet, Archibald Macleish. And in 1936 he launched the fantastically successful *Life* picture magazine, which nearly bankrupted his outfit because its circulation so rapidly outstripped its advertising rates that it lost five million dollars before the journalistic gusher could be brought under control. Other publications, film, radio, and television enterprises have been included in the Luce empire but the big money-makers are *Time*, with a "readership" (original circulation plus pass-on readers) of over three million a week and about one hundred million dollars of gross revenue a year, and *Life*, with "readership" of twenty-six million and another hundred million dollars of gross annual earnings. The monthly total net circulation of all the Luce magazines is over thirty million—and that means power as well as money. This impressive journalistic success was made in its essentials before Harry Luce was forty years old.

More impressive is the fact that the greatest growth came after the death of Harry's friend, partner, and co-genius, Briton Hadden, in 1929. It was to be six years before Harry found another publishing partner of equal brilliance, when he married Clare Boothe Brokaw, herself a skilled magazine editor and successful playwright. In fact, the marriage of this meteoric woman and this monolithic publisher gave rise to the comment that, as usual, when an irresistible force meets an immovable object, they marry. At any rate, Luce divorced the wife of his youth and the mother of his two sons, the lovely Lila Holtz of St. Louis, whom he had met in Rome in 1921 when he was still a student at Oxford.

Tall, well set-up, with thinning sandy hair, gray eyes and a slight stammer, at the age of 55 Harry Luce is, as many really shy men are, rather blunt and even aggressive in manner. He is often regarded as a ruthless self-made so-and-so but he is no penny-pincher and the proverbial munificence of his salary scale has driven many of his editors into premature stomach ulcers.

His outlook on world affairs has been deeply colored by his Chinese background. He was the first important publisher to speak out for a bolder and more expert policy toward China. While he has never been an "Asia-first" man, he has agreed heartily with Lenin and Stalin that the fate of the world will be decided in Asia. He has strong opinions on practically every part of the globe and his magazines frequently express themselves so vigorously that foreign governments bar their circulation. His general attitude is one of simple American nationalism, coupled with a semi-mystical sense of manifest destiny, a belief that America can save and manage the world in what he called "The American Century"—this one. He is not a political imperialist but he is, very definitely, a moral imperialist who sincerely holds that the spiritual values of American life are positive goods which can regenerate mankind.

He belongs in the New Republican Party as surely as do Eisenhower, Duff, and Dewey. Like them, he is an old-stock American with deep Colonial roots. Like them, he was brought up in modest circumstances, made his way by his own native ability, and achieved outstanding success in free competition. Like them, he believes in the basic virtues and in human character as the key to national salvation. Like them, he has a strong missionary impulse. He has seen and known much of the world and believes that America can yet save the human race from sin and death. Next to Dewey himself, he has contributed more in brains and manpower to this administration than any other member of the Eisenhower team.

More important still, he has learned his own limitations and confines his political energies to the channel of his publications. In 1950, there was talk of having him run for the United States Senate in Connecticut and he seriously considered a political career. But his publishing associates objected: "Harry," they told him, "you're a damn good publisher but you may be a lousy Senator. You don't know whether you could be elected. Why jeopardize your magazines by getting into a game you don't understand?" He blinked, swallowed and accepted their advice—one of the few American publishers on record who has passed by the catnip of political office and has stuck to his own line.

5. Two Generals

Two regular army generals, one willingly and the other against his will, made a decisive contribution to Eisenhower's campaign. Both had exchanged their khaki uniforms for the striped pants of Big Business, both were notably successful commanders and organizers, and both were originally engineer officers, members of the aristocracy of brains in the West Point–army hierarchy. The first was a trim, incisive Georgian named Lucius D. Clay. The second was a spare, baldish, and dramatic native of Arkansas by the name of Douglas MacArthur.

Lucius Clay was seven years younger than "Ike" and

had graduated from West Point two years after him, in 1918. He promptly married his "one and only," Marjorie McKeown, who is still his wife and the mother of two grown sons. Clay was born of an old southern family in the little town of Marietta, Georgia, the state which supplied the famous Confederate General "Dutch" Longstreet. He is an exemplar of the old southern tradition of military service to the nation.

His career at first was that of a competent young engineer officer. It took him thirty years of service all over the world to rise to the rank of general. For sixteen of those years he lived and raised two sons on the pay of a first lieutenant. He was always regarded as brilliant and at one time taught engineering at West Point. Then he was assigned to the vital training school of military logistics, the rivers and harbors work of the army engineers. In 1937, he was called out to Manila to serve with Eisenhower on MacArthur's Philippine staff. A year later he was recalled to build the great Red River Dam in Texas. After a brief tour of duty in organizing the defense airport program for the Civil Aeronautics Authority, he was brought into the War Department, where he became deputy chief of staff in charge of the army's two hundred billion dollar materials procurement program. In 1945 he was made deputy to Eisenhower and a year later became Deputy Military Governor of Occupied Germany; he was promoted to command of all United States troops in Germany in 1947.

Scarcely had he received this last post when the Russians, in retaliation against the Marshall Plan's threat to finance the economic recovery of Europe without Soviet permission, blockaded West Berlin. Amid a welter of confusing instructions from a chaotic administration at Washington, Clay made and announced his dramatic decision that America would never be driven from her rightful place in Berlin. For his startling countermove, the famous Berlin airlift, he was solely and personally responsible. During the six months of the Russian blockade, from April 1st to September 30th, Clay astounded the military world by transporting more than two million tons of food and fuel in British and American planes to the relief of the beleaguered city. This feat made both military and political history and marked Clay as one of the finest organizers in the annals of the American Army.

Then, late in 1949, he returned to New York City and accepted the position of chairman and general manager of the great Continental Can Company, in which capacity—by the way—he raised that concern's sales to a record figure of four hundred and seventy-five million dollars in 1952. Dewey had admired Clay in the course of a trip to Occupied Germany and West Berlin in 1949, and asked him to take another job, that of unsalaried Chairman of the New York State Civil Defense Commission. Clay accepted, as a matter of course, and went to work so unobtrusively that the governor did not see him again for a number of months until it was time for the backstage planning for "Ike's" nomination. Clay became the tactful contact man and military intermediary between the clandestine "Draft Ike" headquarters in the Hotel Commodore and Eisenhower's SHAPE command near Paris. He also did discreet missionary work for "Ike" among the Big Business executives who were inclined at first to favor Senator Taft.

The association between the two men was close and friendly and contributed to the smooth handling of the difficult problem involved in nominating a big man who wasn't there and who had long refrained from giving any public or private assurance that he would run if nominated or serve if elected.

Not long after his inauguration, Eisenhower told a luncheon guest that he had not really wanted to be President but that his friends had taken charge until the draft got out of hand and could no longer be controlled. Lucius Clay was in fact the chief of "Ike's" army friends involved in this operation. Whereas the Big Brass "who knew Ike when—" were visibly disturbed at the prospect of having a President who really knew the inner workings of Pentagon procurement, this efficient Georgian selflessly placed himself at the service of his old commander and worked for his political success.

In this he provided a curious contrast with "Ike's" old commander, General of the Army Douglas MacArthur.

MacArthur was born and bred in the old army of the Indian fighting and the Spanish-American War. As the son of General Arthur MacArthur, he first saw the light in 1880 on an army post in Arkansas. Too young to fight in the war with Spain, he graduated from West Point in 1903, at the head of his class, and entered the prize corps of engineers as a second lieutenant.

Of his military and political promise there could be no doubt from the very start. His career fully justified his early brilliance: service in the Philippines, military aide to "Teddy" Roosevelt, a part in Wilson's famous Vera Cruz expedition, assignment to the General Staff at Washington, infantry service in France in the first World War, during which he was twice wounded in action, duty with the Army of Occupation in Germany, appointment as Commandant of Cadets at West Point, elevation to the post of Army Chief of Staff from 1930 to 1935, retirement to the Philippines in 1935, and a continuous record of historic military and political actions in the Far Pacific from that time until his abrupt recall from Tokyo by President Truman on April 11th, 1951 for dissenting from the administration's policy on the Korean War.

There is no need to appraise, despise, or exalt that great record; it speaks for itself and his achievement as supreme commander of the allied occupation forces in Japan was so outstanding that he must be credited with having made great contributions to Japan's reconciliation with the West in the Japanese peace treaty which Dulles negotiated six months after MacArthur's enforced removal from his high command.

For some eight years MacArthur was regarded as potential Presidential material. In 1944, Senator Vandenberg of Michigan took a trip to MacArthur's Australian headquarters at Brisbane to canvass his "availability" for the campaign against Roosevelt.

At that time he was unavailable and also suffered from an inter-service feud of long standing with the navy. So persistent was this feud that in 1942, during the doomed defense of Bataan Peninsula, President Roosevelt was compelled to send tactful orders to remind MacArthur on Corregidor that at least *some* navy men were entitled to citations and decorations for gallantry.

In 1948, MacArthur's name was entered in the Republican primary in Wisconsin, his adopted state, but the showing was a disappointment. However, the drama of the Korean War, the desperate fighting around Pusan, the daring Inchon landings, and the back-and-forth surge of the armies to the Yalu and back again and then north once more to the 38th Parallel, placed the general in the most favorable limelight. Quite naturally in one of his age—he was 72—he also tended to regard Eisenhower as a man who had been his subordinate and "ghostwriter," as not his equal for the Presidency of the United States.

Riding a wave of public distaste for the ungracious manner of his recall, MacArthur soon became part of the

"Stop Eisenhower" movement; the skilled politicians
promoting Taft gave assurances that "Mac" was their
reserve candidate if "Mr. Republican" failed to win the
nomination. The opening days of the Republican Convention at Chicago witnessed a strange transplanting of
the old Hitlerian military mystique from Nuremberg to
the Stockyards: drum-taps and bugle calls, and repeated
mass pledges of allegiance to the flag, culminating in the
arrival of MacArthur himself, slender in civilian clothes,
modest, quiet, and unassuming, to deliver the keynote
speech. This was expected to be as dramatic and electri-
fying as Bryan's famous "Cross of Gold" speech in 1896
and to produce a political stampede for Douglas Mac-
Arthur. It was a good speech, as all of his speeches are,
but it was a political anti-climax. When it was over, he
was over, too. He had lived too long outside the country
and was too old to speak to or for the present generation
of Americans. He was warmly applauded and swiftly
forgotten. The Eisenhower forces rode through to a
first-ballot victory for "Ike" and General MacArthur became a Big Business executive as Chairman of Reming-
ton-Rand.

He had, however, made an important if unintentional
contribution to Eisenhower's victory. His prolonged
Presidential "availability" had helped prepare public
opinion for the election of a professional soldier as chief
executive for the first time in eighty years. And the
drama of his recall from Japan had given the Republican

Party a major campaign issue in the form of general dissatisfaction with the administration's self-defeating stalemate policy in Korea. MacArthur did not offer Eisenhower any assistance in the campaign nor was he asked to, but "Ike" harbored no hard feelings and, after the election, promptly consulted him on the course to follow in the Far East, where MacArthur had served so long and so brilliantly in war and in peace. For MacArthur, the somewhat effulgent orator and the old soldier who could not die and would not fade away, provided a perfect foil for the younger general, whose brilliance was less marked but whose sense of comradeship was strong enough to overlook past differences for the sake of political solidarity and national unity.

III

ALL THE KING'S MEN

1. Sherman Adams

EVERY President is more than a single individual. In his political and executive actions, he is a composite of himself and his immediate staff. Thus Franklin Roosevelt was a tincture of Louis Howe, Marvin McIntyre, Eleanor Roosevelt, Steve Early, Sam Rosenman, and Harry Hopkins. So was Mr. Truman a mixture of himself, Matt Connelly, Clark Clifford, Harry Vaughan, and John Snyder.

The White House staff of Presidential intimates can develop along one of two lines. They can serve, as they served Roosevelt until his illness in 1944, as avenues to channel information into the President, or as a Palace Guard, such as surrounded Truman, determined to fend off outsiders and to "air-condition" the chief executive with only such information and contacts as they wish him to have.

In the case of Eisenhower, the White House staff so

far has fallen into neither of these categories. It is, in fact, a kind of composite political brain including three members of the "Dewey Team," and other aides trained and tested by the actual political campaign which elected "Ike" President.

Chief of staff for this operating unit is former Governor Sherman Adams of New Hampshire. Fifty-four years old, slight and taciturn, Governor Adams, like many successful New Englanders, does not look his part at all. He might be a moderately well-to-do owner of a couple of Gloucester fishing schooners instead of possessing a rather remarkable record for achievement in both business and politics. He is the man who conducts the regular 8:30 o'clock morning White House staff meetings and directs the traffic of reports in and out of the President's oval study. A sensible, even-tempered man, a cross between David Harum and Henry Thoreau, he began as "Ike's" 1952 political lucky piece and ended as the pivot man in the Eisenhower group.

His first direct connection with the Eisenhower movement began with the famous New Hampshire Presidential primary of March 11th, 1952—the first and hence the crucial test of "Ike's" standing with Republican voters. New Hampshire's twelve delegates to the nominating convention were at stake and the Taft forces were pouring in money and energy in an attempt to upset "Ike's" bandwagon before it started rolling. Dewey sent Tom Stephens up to Concord to work with Adams and the whole nation watched while the "Ike-likers" had an attack of underconfidence and the Taft-addicts became correspondingly optimistic. But when the votes were counted, all twelve Eisenhower delegates had been elected, by a vote of forty-six to thirty-four thousand, in an intensively conservative Republican constituency. At this point, Governor Adams unobtrusively strolled into the center of the Eisenhower group and has stayed there ever since. He acted as "Ike's" floor manager at the Chicago convention and then as manager of the staff at Denver headquarters and on the campaign train, and was in charge of the Eisenhower offices at the Hotel Commodore after the election. Unless he decides to try for a seat in the United States Senate, now that he is no longer governor, there is every prospect that this shrewd, dry-humored man of great affairs will stay on in the White House as long as "Ike" is President.

Sherman Adams' whole career is, in itself, an almost perfect illustration of the basic character of the Republican resurrection. A descendant of the primeval Henry Adams who founded the famous Massachusetts family which has so far included two American Presidents, Sherman Adams was born in East Dover, Vermont, early in 1899. Soon afterward, his parents moved to Providence, Rhode Island, where he attended the public schools before entering Dartmouth College in 1916. Two years later he enlisted in the Marine Corps in World War I, but returned to college after the armistice and graduated in 1920.

The following fall he went into the lumber business. Fond of outdoor life, he rose from the ranks as scaler, lumber surveyor, foreman, plant manager, and finally manager of timberland operations for the Black River Lumber Company in Vermont. In 1923, he married a Vermont girl, Rachel White, and is the father of four children—three girls and a boy.

Up to 1940, his life might almost have been invented by the Thornton Wilder of *Our Town*. An Episcopalian, at one time he sang for a year in the choir of Washington's National Cathedral. He is director of several trade associations, a director of the Pemigewasset National Bank of Plymouth, New Hampshire, and of the Pemigewasset Railroad. He is also a member of the executive committee of the Society for the Protection of New Hampshire Forests, an honorary member of the Ammonoosuc Fire Wardens, a member of the New England Council and of the American Legion. He also belongs to the Masons, Mystic Shrine, Elks, Moose, the Grange and the Grafton County Farm Bureau. He has raised funds for the U.S.O., Russian Relief, and Navy Relief. He is a friendly, persistent joiner of good causes and fraternal organizations.

Adams was over forty when he first got mixed up in politics. Running as a Republican in the town of Lincoln, which was Democratic by nearly three to one, he was elected to the New Hampshire state legislature by a large majority. When he ran for re-election in 1942, he received the undivided vote of Lincoln and was chosen unanimously as speaker of the house in 1943. The following year he was elected to Congress from New Hampshire's second district and specialized on flood control and labor legislation.

His first political setback came in 1946 when he was defeated in the Republican primary for the governorship of New Hampshire. So he took a couple of years out in the pulp and paper industry and won the governorship in 1948. New Hampshire is a stubborn political community, but Adams made substantial progress in modernizing the state's administration. However, the Yankees in the legislature refused to vote the new taxes needed to finance his program, so Adams calmly turned around and instituted a general retrenchment in the cost of state government which was calculated to make the opponents of taxation realize that economy also has few charms for the practical politician. Then along came the Eisenhower movement and Sherman Adams swung himself aboard with the casual ease of a New Englander hopping aboard a train on his polysyllabic railroad.

Adams' contribution to "Ike's" White House operation is both moral and practical, if such a distinction can be made in politics. He is a good executive who is careful not to stand between the President and his subordinates whenever the latter need to see "Ike." With an orderly mind and a sense of business management, he keeps the papers moving across the executive desk and the staff busy on their assignments. He is also a center of unhurried common sense in the midst of great events. That is perhaps his greatest value, a permanent patch of sunny calm in the center of the storm.

2. THOMAS E. STEPHENS

It would be almost impossible to find anyone more different in background and temperament from Sherman Adams than his old partner in the New Hampshire primary fight, the present White House Special Counsel and Acting Appointment Secretary, Thomas E. Stephens.

But just as Governor Adams' job is one of the most burdensome in the new Republican Administration, Tom Stephens' role involves a continuous and nerve-wracking responsibility for organizing the details of the President's working day. He serves as the valve which regulates the flow of official and unofficial visitors to the impressive oval-shaped office which is the nerve center of the government. Upon Stephens' judgment, to a great extent, depends the orderly handling of the most important schedule in the world and the good relations of the President with leaders of Congress and business and many powerful national organizations.

Stephens, a slim, dark lawyer in his late forties, was born and raised in Ireland. He has an unpredictable Irish wit and a fund of humorous anecdotes which has enabled him to relieve tension at the White House, much as it did in his previous political associations. Stephens' father brought him to this country at the time of the Easter Rebellion and the execution of Sir Roger Casement when young Tom was thirteen.

As so often happens with the Irish when they emigrate, he almost automatically became a politician. What was extraordinary in Tom's case was that he became a Republican politician in Democratic Brooklyn. Perhaps it was only a refinement of the Irish tradition to be "agin the government." In any case, Stephens happened to become a precocious and successful operator in politics.

He was twenty-eight years old when he received his law degree from Brooklyn Law School. That was in 1932; in the same year he was appointed as Assistant Corporation Counsel of the City of New York and assigned to Albany, where he represented the city's interest in matters before the state legislature.

Then he served for a number of years as assistant to the president of New York City's Council during the Republican reform administration of the mid-thirties. He took time out from politics during World War II to put in nearly three years of overseas service as major in the Air Force in the European theater, most of this time in Italy.

He returned to become an aide to Herbert Brownell, now Attorney General, in the conduct of the 1948 Presidential campaign of Thomas E. Dewey. Brownell used him with great success as a troubleshooter and as advance man for the pre-convention primary contests around the country. Stephens had resumed the private practice of law, but politics made continual intrusions into his profession. When John Foster Dulles was appointed by Dewey to fill the Senate seat vacated by Robert F. Wagner, Sr., Tom came along as political secretary. Mr. Dulles was defeated for election to the post in 1949, but he liked Stephens so well that, when chosen for Secretary of State, he vied with the President for the competent young lawyer's services, offering him one of the top spots in the State Department.

Stephens is a natural-born idea man and something of a worrier. According to what can best be called internal evidence, he probably would have been an advertising genius. While he missed going into that field, he fell victim to the advertising man's occupational ailment—ulcers. After many years of intense suffering, he submitted to an operation which amputated a large part of his stomach. Now the ulcers are gone, but his lean and hungry look and the necessity for taking six meals instead of the normal three testify to the resultant impairment of his digestive equipment.

Although he is a stimulating and cheerful member of any group he chances to be with, business or social, he betrays at times an extreme pessimism. This is particularly true in things political, and may be merely the product of the many years of Republican reverses in the pre-Eisenhower era in New York.

For example, at the January 20th, 1953 inaugural of the general, Governor Dewey bumped into Stephens. Tom was sedate, proper, and extremely restrained in acknowledging the warm greetings of his many friends among the celebrating party big-wigs. To Dewey he cautiously commented as the new President reviewed his inaugural parade: "You know, Governor, I am now about willing to agree this fellow Eisenhower is going to get the nomination."

His theory of politics is simple and practical: take care of the details. As a test of his theory, in early 1946 when he was director of the campaign division of the Republican National Committee, he once scored an impressive upset and elected a Republican Congressman in a "sure" Democratic Pennsylvania District. His first job on reaching New Hampshire for the primary was to take charge of having an Eisenhower banner stretched across the main street in the state capital. At the Chicago convention he was credited with the ingenious trick, which infuriated the Taftites, of having a loud-speaker truck circle the Conrad Hilton Hotel, blaring piously: "Help us keep Chicago clean! Please do not litter the sidewalks with your used Taft buttons!" This, however, he emphatically denies. His work with Governor Driscoll at

Trenton, New Jersey paid off in another major Eisenhower victory, when "Ike" beat Taft by over one hundred and fifty thousand votes. When Eisenhower returned to the United States in June, Tom was promptly
assigned as the general's appointment secretary and
served as such during the entire campaign.

With Stephens screening "Ike's" visitors and Jim
Hagerty handling his press relations, there might have
been some feeling among the Taftites that Dewey had
too firm a grip on White House mechanics or Tom himself may have found the steady grind of the appointment
job too much for his truncated digestive equipment. At
any rate, "Ike" named him as White House Special
Counsel, the job previously held by Clark Clifford and
Charlie Murphy under Truman, and put Arthur Vandenberg, Jr. in charge of the appointments. However,
the son of the late Michigan statesman became ill and
did not assume his White House assignment. Tom never
was relieved of the responsibility for the Eisenhower
calling list, despite the fact that the Commission signed
by the President indicated that he was to be the White
House lawyer.

Tom Stephens contributes an unconventional approach to politics and an original mind. He is not only a
competent lawyer who for many years was a member of
successful law firms in New York and Washington; he
is also fascinated by all kinds of inventions.

Stephens always has one or two hobbies going at full speed and a couple more in the planning stage. On impulse, he once bought a farm in Virginia in partnership with another lawyer with an equally meager agricultural background. They sold it just before Tom entered the White House after a fling at absentee raising of watermelons, pine trees, pigs, sheep, and ducks. The livestock for the farm was obtained by tossing a neighboring farmer "double or nothing" for them. Subsequently, he took to growing mushrooms in a closet of his Washington apartment. People said it could not be done. A small circle of friends say that so far his crops have been good —no toadstools.

Tom Stephens may be an amateur at raising farm products but he is an old pro at bringing in a harvest at the polls. He learned how elections are won and lost in Manhattan Island, one of the toughest political battlegrounds in the nation. The midtown district where Stephens and Brownell and Dewey received their political baptism and much of their training was one of the few Republican islands in the New Deal seas during the 'thirties and 'forties. He has rung doorbells, watched polling places, observed and advised state legislatures, managed city and state campaigns. His political "savvy" and keen understanding of people are valuable assets, indeed, to the President, who is the first to admit his own lack of experience in the rough-and-tumble political game.

3. Gabriel Hauge

Next in order to join the Eisenhower group was Dr. Gabriel Hauge, a Minnesota-born economist in his early forties. A serious, heavy-built man, fair-haired and blue-eyed, Hauge is a man of Norwegian ancestry, the son of a Lutheran clergyman in the little prairie town of Hawley, Minnesota, where "Gabe" was born.

Hauge possesses a clear, thorough kind of honest mind which has carried him far and high in a competitive society. He graduated from co-educational Concord College in Minnesota in 1935. The following year he served as its assistant dean of men, moving on to Harvard Business School, which gave him a master's degree in economics in 1938. Nine years later, Harvard gave him his Ph.D. After graduating from the Business School he was appointed budget examiner in the Minnesota state budget bureau. The same fall he returned to Harvard, where he taught economics for two years and then moved on to Princeton for another two years, also as an instructor in economics. He put in a summer vacation as senior statistician in the Federal Reserve Bank of New York the year which witnessed the outbreak of World War II.

After Pearl Harbor he promptly enlisted in the navy and put in a four-year stretch as a lieutenant-commander on the U.S.S. *California* in the Pacific theater. On being demobilized in 1946, he returned to New York, where Dewey's banking commissioner, Elliott Bell, promptly grabbed him and made him chief of the State Banking Department's Division of Research and Statistics. When Bell left the state government to enter the great McGraw-Hill publishing house in 1950, he brought Hauge along to write the editorials on *Business Week*.

In the meantime, Hauge had married attractive Helen Resor of Greenwich, Connecticut, a member of the great J. Walter Thompson advertising family. The young couple have four children—including one set of twin sons as well as two daughters. On the birth of the twins, he stubbornly resisted the argument of his friends that he should pass out two cigars instead of one. He is a devoted, solid family man as well as a rock-like, level-headed man of affairs.

While recognizing Elliott Bell's prior claim on Hauge's services, Governor Dewey kept his eye on this extremely competent and loyal lieutenant. Dewey repeatedly made use of Hauge's services in the preparation of state papers and economic research. Both as a research man and as a speech writer, Hauge had the important duty of supplying ballast and balance. He would never hesitate to weigh the facts carefully before agreeing to any line of political argument.

This kind of intellectual integrity is hard on the average politician, but Dewey and others who worked with Gabe found it invaluable. Honesty in thought, as well as scrupulous care in expressing it accurately, are rare in politics and that was what Hauge had to offer. In addition, his own economic philosophy was entirely in tune with that of the New Republicans. As became his Scandinavian blood, he believed in the "middle way" which "Ike" was later to proclaim, avoiding both the Scylla of unbridled individualism and the Charybdis of Marxist mass management.

Early in 1952, Dewey pre-empted Hauge's spare time and energies and set him to work in the temporary Eisenhower headquarters at New York's Hotel Commodore, in charge of research. Hampered by lack of funds and of his own time, the young Minnesotan went steadily to work and had much of the basic material needed for an orderly Eisenhower campaign. Then, when "Ike" returned from Europe, Hauge automatically moved into "Ike's" campaign staff—at Denver, at Chicago, in New York, and on the train—as economic consultant.

Directly after his inauguration, Eisenhower appointed Hauge as his administrative assistant, with the special task of passing on all economic matters. Since, at least in the opinion of professional economists, practically everything in modern government has an economic angle, this is a pretty large assignment. Hauge soon discovered that his office in the east wing of the White House was too crowded and noisy. He had the calm foresight to collar a large, air-cooled sub-cathedral on the second floor of the old State-War-Navy Building, right next to the Budget Bureau; this location has the added advantage of being nearer to the President's of-

fice than was his old room over by the Treasury on East
Executive Avenue.

He has taken a house up near the National Cathedral,
moved wife and children down from New York, and is
prepared to work on national and world affairs just as
methodically as he used to work on his classroom lectures
at Princeton or on his editorials for *Business Week.* His
position and responsibility are, roughly, those of the former chairman of the Board of Economic Advisers, the
highly vocal Dr. Leon Keyserling, but without the title
and, above all, without the publicity. Economic competence and intellectual honesty may not save the world or
the nation but they can help and, so long as he can be
helpful, Gabe Hauge will stay and do his job, without
fanfare, complaint, or public recognition.

4. James C. Hagerty

The remaining member of the Dewey trio to leave
Albany in order to help "Ike" get to the White House is
a freckled and bespectacled ex-newspaperman who was
born in Plattsburg, New York shortly after William
Howard Taft became President of the United States.

James C. Hagerty has undertaken the man-killing job
of White House press secretary at the age of forty-four,
and is giving "Ike" the same dogged service and journalistic common sense he previously gave Tom Dewey at
Albany for over ten years.

Plattsburg is famous for three things: it was the scene of Commodore Macdonough's naval victory over a British flotilla in the War of 1812; it witnessed the volunteer officers training school organized by General Leonard Wood in 1915 to help prepare for World War I; and it was the journalistic cradle of "Old Jim"—James A. Hagerty, since 1922 the political expert of the New York *Times*.

Both "Old Jim" and "Young Jim" retain the Irish flair for political quick-wittedness which guarantees a free ringside seat at any political show.

Young Jim Hagerty never expected to enter politics. He intended to be a newspaperman, like his father. After preparing at New Jersey's Blair Academy, he went on to Columbia University, from which he graduated in 1934. As an undergraduate, he had acted as campus correspondent for the *Times* and on graduating—with no nonsense about attending that trade school for publicity men known as the Columbia School of Journalism—he went straight into the city room of New York's most distinguished morning newspaper. The *Times* city room is a post-graduate course in applied journalism and, after a four-year grind on police reporting, general reporting, and rewrite, young Hagerty was sent to Albany as his paper's legislative correspondent.

That was in 1938, the year of Dewey's first and all but successful bid for the governorship. Jim stayed on as the *Times* man in Albany until 1943, covering Dewey's victorious campaign in 1942. He was completely taken by surprise when the first Republican to be chosen governor of New York in twenty years turned around and offered him the job of handling his press relations at Albany. After some hesitation, Jim accepted and remained a member of Dewey's staff until Eisenhower's victory compelled him to pull up stakes in Albany and move on to Washington.

Life in Albany suited Jim right down to the ground. Essentially a small-town upstate boy, he loves to play golf, shooting in the middle eighties, and he enjoys the feel of New York state politics.

Politics was in his Irish blood but he caught golf the way some people catch epilepsy. It happened at Colorado Springs in the summer of 1943, when he was covering Dewey's pre-convention activities. Dewey was laid up for a few days; to kill time Jim decided to try golf for the first time. He immediately became a passionate, inveterate, and devoted golfer, a man who swings a club not always well but extremely hard, and even succeeded in communicating this dread disease to his wife. When he moved to Washington one of his first thoughts was to locate a house not far from the Chevy Chase Country Club. In 1950, when Dewey planned to retire as governor and practice law, he began to disband his "team." Elliott Bell left the Banking Department for McGraw-Hill, John Burton left the Budget Bureau to become chairman of the State Power Authority, and Dewey's

Secretary, Paul Lockwood, was moved onto the Public Service Commission. For the remainder of his term, Dewey promoted Jim to fill Lockwood's place, but kept him still on his old press-relations assignment. Then public pressure compelled Dewey to seek a third four-year term as governor and Hagerty stayed on as his secretary until June of 1952, when he was lent to Eisenhower.

By then, Jim was an experienced hand in national politics. He had served as Dewey's press secretary in both the 1944 and 1948 Presidential campaigns. He had also worked intimately with the dynamic governor on national speeches and public policies. Liked and trusted by Albany and Washington correspondents, Hagerty was the inevitable choice to handle press matters for "Ike," before and at the convention and during the campaign.

His move to Washington meant more than a revolution in residence. His whole pattern of living was altered, and for the better, by the general's old-fashioned preference for early rising and early retiring. Dewey is a late worker who thinks nothing of keeping himself and his staff on the job until two or three in the morning. Then he gets a respectable amount of sleep and shows up in the office somewhere around eleven o'clock. Now that Hagerty has to show at the White House by 8 A.M., it is almost as much of a strain on his habits as if he had joined the staff on an afternoon paper.

A deceptively solemn man, his poker face often breaks into a mischievous grin; he is a hard kidder, "dead-pan," but his tongue carries no sting. His contribution to Eisenhower, apart from his personal familiarity with the mechanics of the job and his wide friendship with newspapermen, is his ability to insist on that part of our traditional "decent respect for the opinion of mankind" which is represented by the pressure of a free press. Particularly in dealing with the army, where commanders frequently put their trust in censorship, it is valuable for "Ike" to have a man around who knows the other side of newsgathering and can judge fairly what should be told and what can safely be withheld in matters of public information.

While still on the *Times*, Jim married Marjorie Lucas. They are in the tradition of the New Republicans, still married and have two sons, the oldest of whom is at Hamilton College preparing for a commission in the Marine Corps while the younger will go to college in a couple of years.

To help him in his White House press job, Jim reached out and grabbed Murray Snyder, former Albany correspondent for the New York *Herald-Tribune*. This selection gives a measure of Hagerty's sound political judgment. Snyder is young, able, and highly-respected in the newspaper world, which is fine. Equally fortunate is the fact that Snyder has served a rock-ribbed Republican paper, whereas Jim's newspaper connections were with an independent Democratic daily. So the political books are neatly balanced in terms of New York journalism and Jim got the services of a first-rate assistant into the bargain.

5. EMMET JOHN HUGHES

There are other significant White House appointments in addition to Sherman Adams and the Dewey trio —men like young Vandenberg of Michigan; General Wilton B. Persons of Alabama, the Georgia Tech graduate who joined the Coast Artillery in the first World War and rose to become the army's ace public-relations officer and Congressional contact man; and Governor Val Peterson of Nebraska, who spent a few days as "Ike's" administrative assistant after both Nebraska senators had vindictively blackballed him as ambassador to India.

But perhaps as important an appointment as any was "Ike's" selection of Emmet J. Hughes, text editor of *Life*, as principal Presidential speech writer.

The art of political ghost-writing is a delicate, difficult and thankless one. If things go badly you are blamed; if they go well, you become the target for intrigue and jealousy. The job calls for two entirely contradictory qualifications: an intimate and masterful awareness of the whole political situation and a selfless subordination of the writer to the character, personality, and convictions of the man whose speeches he drafts. This combination of statesmanship and humility is not easily found. For example, Roosevelt used and discarded a whole stable of

ghost-writers: Ray Moley, Stanley High, Tom Corcoran, Bob Sherwood, and always Sam Rosenman. Truman set up an oratorical assembly line, feeding the raw
material in a steady flow to his immediate operators, Clifford or Connelly, before standing up and delivering the
finished product. Dewey works hard and often exhaust-
ing hours on every speech he delivers, usually in close
consultation with as many as seven or eight specialists,
writers, and advisers.

But Dewey actually dictates and edits every speech he
delivers, usually through three or more drafts, and in the
case of his book, *Journey to the Far Pacific,* he wrote an
average of four drafts of every chapter and worked on
it personally far into the night in addition to doing his
exacting job as governor.

When General Eisenhower returned shortly before
the Republican Convention, the ghost-writing situation
was naturally nebulous. "Ike's" own public-relations officers were army-minded and out of their element in
dealing with American politics. At first, Dr. Stanley
High of *The Reader's Digest* was assigned to work with
the general, but as the campaign got tough someone was
needed who shared High's ideals and also understood
brass knuckles. There was only one place to go for that:
to Harry Luce. Luce promptly produced C. D. Jackson
of *Fortune* to handle speech-assembly operations at
"Ike's" Hotel Commodore headquarters, and Emmet J.
Hughes of *Life* to accompany the candidate and fit the

prefabricated New York output into the political picture of the moment.

Only thirty-one years old and the son of a district court judge in Summit, New Jersey, Hughes has an extensive grounding in both propaganda and intelligence work. He graduated from Princeton, Phi Beta Kappa, *summa cum laude*, and with honors in modern European history, in June of 1941. That same fall he went on to do graduate work at Columbia but, after Pearl Harbor, abandoned his studies to join the Elmer Davis Office of War Information. A devout Catholic, he was appropriately shipped to Madrid in August of 1942 and remained there until May of 1946. In an effort to escape into active military service, he enlisted in the army in Algiers as a private, but was promptly sent back to Madrid, where he continued to work for OWI, the State Department, and military intelligence, winning a special intelligence citation for "exceptional loyalty and devotion to duty." After his discharge, he joined the staff of *Time*, which sent him as bureau chief, first to Rome and then to Berlin during the period of the Russian blockade. Back in New York again in 1949, he was appointed text editor of *Life*. There he remained until early September of 1952, when he was granted leave of absence to join Eisenhower as a speech writer.

Emmet Hughes is a scholarly man with an incisive mind and a preference for simple, direct vivid writing. He collects Goya etchings, reads detective stories, and plays a moderately good game of golf. He is the author of two fairly good books, *The Church and the Liberal Society*, which was a Catholic Book Club selection, and *Report from Spain*, published in 1947, which earned him the following "rave" from *The Saturday Review of Literature*:

> "Hughes has a logical, penetrating mind, a precise workmanlike respect for accuracy, a mature political judgment solidly based on a thorough academic foundation, and an objectivity limited only by a fervent respect for the dignity and freedom of man."

His was a *Life* marriage since, in the course of his editorial researches, he made the acquaintance of a pretty *Life* researcher named Eileen Lanouette. After exchanging notes, they decided to continue their research together and were married. Their daughter, Mary Larkin Hughes, was born a week before Eisenhower's election.

Benjamin Disraeli once said, "With words we govern man." Hughes is "Ike's" word expert, but words of themselves can mean no more than the man who writes them intends them to mean. Sincerity, in the last analysis, is the great bond which holds Eisenhower and his team together. Hughes could not write a word for Eisenhower which "Ike" does not believe or that Hughes does not also believe. That is one secret of successful ghost-writing. The other is that Hughes knows what to say. He rounds out a smooth-running, first-class White House staff.

IV

THE STRIPED PANTAGON

1. A RECEIVERSHIP IN FOREIGN POLICY

THE New Republicans are the receivers in bankruptcy of the foreign policies they have inherited. At the turn of the century, as a nation we more or less unconsciously married ourselves to the British fleet and nation. This was a period when the British fleet held the peace of the world, but our timing was bad. It was on the very eve of another period when the submarine and airplane were about to challenge the basis of British sea power. It was also on the very eve of an era when the rising tide of Asian and Arab nationalism threatened the foundations of the whole world-order.

As a result, the Republican receivers in bankruptcy for fifty years of American foreign policy must try to balance some startling and contradictory entries in our diplomatic ledger:

China: We started the century with a determination to maintain Chinese territorial and political integrity; we insisted at Yalta in 1945 that China should break the Nine-Power Treaty of 1922, which had affirmed our traditional Far Eastern policy, in favor of the Soviet Union.

Japan: We backed Japan against Russia in 1904–5; we almost went to war with Japan over China in 1921; we befriended her for a decade and then drifted into a Japanese war which ended in our again befriending, defending, and financing this beaten Asian nation.

Germany: Theodore Roosevelt used our traditional friendship for Germany to counterbalance British claims on our diplomatic support. Woodrow Wilson brought us into war against Germany in 1917. We supported the German Weimar Republic and financed German reparations in the 1920's; we boycotted and eventually fought Hitler's Germany; today we are befriending, defending, and financing the West German Bonn Republic.

Russia: For most of the nineteenth century, we were firm friends with Czarist Russia. Czar Alexander mediated with the British to gain us a favorable peace after the War of 1812. During the Civil War, a Russian fleet protected the Pacific Coast against Confederate raiders and another Russian fleet visited New York as a reminder to France and Britain that it could be risky to intervene on behalf of the Confederacy. Then we gradually drifted into hostility to Russia. We resented Russian encroachments in the Far East, backed Japan diplomatically in the Russo-Japanese War of 1904–5, and broke our commercial treaty with Russia out of resentment at Czarist persecution of the Jews. For a short time in 1917 we hailed the Kerensky revolution with enthusiasm but swiftly settled into dislike for, and opposition to, the Communist regime. This opposition lasted until 1933, when Roosevelt recognized the Soviet Government and instituted a policy of friendship which led to outright alliance and support in World War II. Yet by the end of 1945 we resumed our previous opposition to the Soviet Government and gradually appointed ourselves as the protector and protagonist of the free world against Soviet enslavement.

Europe: We ended World War I insisting, under the Wilsonian doctrine of national self-determination, that Europe be divided into small national governments. At the time it was not too inaccurately described as meaning that "every little language got a country all its own." Twenty-five years later, we were insisting with equal sincerity that Western Europe should unite in recompense for our thirty billion dollars of post-war assistance and our treaty obligations under NATO to maintain American troops for the defense of Western Europe against the Soviet threat.

Disarmament: During the 1920's we vigorously urged Europe to disarm; in the 1950's we earnestly pleaded with the European nations to rearm in order to avert catastrophe.

World Government: After the first World War, we proposed and then rejected the League of Nations. Before the second World War had ended, we proposed and joined the United Nations and engaged in war in Korea in the name of this organization.

Latin America: During all these decades of indecision and sharp shifts in national attitude, we have alternately blown hot and cold on Latin America. Theodore Roosevelt and William Howard Taft relied on "dollar diplomacy" and the American navy in the Western Hemisphere. Woodrow Wilson intervened by force in Mexico and in various Caribbean countries, to "shoot men into self-government" and to protect American lives and property. Franklin Roosevelt adopted Elihu Root's "Good Neighbor" policy and poured Federal funds into a program to keep the American Republics quiet during the war against the Axis. President Truman virtually ignored this hemisphere and ignored, also, the ominous spread of native Communist movements in Central and South America.

Party Responsibility: So much for the record, now for the accounting. The Republicans showed great skill and interest in dealing with the Far East and in creating peaceful political and commercial ties with other countries, while every Democratic President in this century involved us in a major war. Yet the responsibility for these wars must be shared by both parties. Theodore Roosevelt started our anti-Japanese policy by sending the American fleet around the world in 1908. Herbert Hoover's Secretary of State announced the so-called "Stimson Doctrine" which by-passed the Nine-Power Treaty and committed us to oppose Japanese territorial gains brought about by force. Both parties cheered when President Truman announced the even more spacious "Truman Doctrine," which asserts our duty to defend every nation against internal as well as external Communist aggression. Intervention in Korea was also cheered by both political parties and has not been disavowed by either.

The task which faces the Republican receivers of an American foreign policy which has collapsed in Eastern Asia, is tottering in Western Europe and the Near East, and is threatened in the Americas, is to substitute a political defense for the costs and risks of purely military postures. The Republican theory has always preferred to create a common material interest between the nations so as to disarm in advance the political antagonisms which precede military hostility. This was the traditional method of British foreign policy during the long, prosperous century between the battle of Waterloo and the first World War. By trade, investment, and the development of backward regions, it was possible to dispel enmity in advance by making our friendship mutually advantageous to all concerned.

Yet it is no longer certain that methods of international conduct which sufficed in the day of the steamship and the electric telegraph will serve as well in the day of the atom and hydrogen bombs, the schnörkel submarine, and the Third International. The force of nationalism has become violently explosive in Asia, all the way from Mukden to New Delhi, and is shaking the Arab world from Teheran to Cairo and from Cairo to Capetown. The evil legacy of American prejudice against the colored races was reinforced by Democratic control of our government and has led to a situation in which the Communists can capitalize to our disadvantage on the rising tide of color throughout three-fourths of the world.

Where fifty years ago we faced as proud republicans a world of monarchy, today we are uneasy, conservative capitalists facing a world of socialism, Communism, flaming nationalism, and profound suspicion of economic and political colonialism. The British Empire itself has lost Asia and is no longer the great world-wide political fact with which we lived in reasonable amity, punctuated by family squabbles, for over a hundred and twenty-five years. The only empire which has expanded during this century is the Russian, which now stretches from the Elbe and the Upper Danube to Shanghai and Canton. France, Austria, Germany, Turkey, Britain, Italy: all other empires shrank or were dismembered. We ourselves were placed in an imperial position but without imperial control, and found ourselves committed to pay annual tribute in men and materials not only to our allies but to our beaten foes.

For the final item in the audit which the Republican receivership must consider is this: after tremendous sacrifices and brilliant military victories in Europe and in Asia, we find ourselves faced with a far greater peril than those dangers which we went to war to overcome. We forgot that good fences make good neighbors. By crushing Germany and Japan, we confronted ourselves with a Soviet Empire which was no longer restrained in Europe or in Asia by powerful neighbors.

2. JOHN FOSTER DULLES

After a lifetime spent in preparing himself for the position, John Foster Dulles became Eisenhower's Secretary of State at the age of sixty-five.

He is the first professional diplomat to head our foreign office since Wilson dismissed Dulles' uncle, Robert Lansing, over thirty years ago. He has entered upon his duties with a grim determination that the State Department shall represent and speak for the American people.

Under his predecessors, thanks to lend-lease and Marshall Plan aid, the State Department often appeared to act as agent for foreign governments, to a degree which undermined its influence both with Congress and the country. A large part of the initial bluntness of Secretary Dulles' approach to the West European governments derived from the need to restore American confidence in the administration's diplomacy.

There are many conflicting views concerning John Foster Dulles. Some regard him as a stiff shirt, others as a reactionary, still others as a man who will "get us into trouble," as though we were not already in trouble. The British complain of his "duplicity" in negotiating the Japanese peace treaty; the Soviets call him a spy and saboteur and accuse him of having started the Korean war!

The truth is that Secretary of State Dulles is part and parcel of the entire Eisenhower Republican movement. He is the son of a Presbyterian minister and was brought up in Watertown, New York. His family was far from wealthy, but his mother's father was John W. Foster, Secretary of State under President Benjamin Harrison, and his uncle was that Robert Lansing who replaced Bryan as Wilson's Secretary of State after the sinking of the *Lusitania*. He came of age and began his successful professional career, after studies at Princeton, the Sorbonne, and George Washington University, before there was any Federal income tax and before the completion of the Panama Canal made us a world power. This was in 1911, when success was measured more by money, and by skill at defending money, than by social position or intellectual attainment.

His attainments were notable. He started practice with the famous international Wall Street law firm of Sullivan & Cromwell. President Wilson used him for negotiations with Panama and other Central American countries, in the effort to hold Latin America in line during our participation in the first World War. He enlisted in the army in 1917 and served as a major on the general staff and later on the War Trade Board. He was one of Wilson's advisers at the Paris peace conference in 1919 and worked with Hoover on European relief.

During the 1920's and 1930's, Dulles became famous for his successful international law practice, and learned the method of personal diplomatic negotiation in twenty years of dealing with foreign agencies and governments. He also traveled in the Far East and interested himself deeply in the work of the Federal Council of Churches, regarding the Christian forces of this country as a vital influence in shaping a just foreign policy.

Toward the close of the second World War, Dulles was a member of the American delegation to the San Francisco Conference, where he helped frame the U.N. Charter. He also served as American delegate at the U.N. Assembly sessions in 1946, '47, '48, and '50.

In 1944, when Dewey initiated the bipartisan foreign policy, he sent Dulles to confer with Secretary of State Hull in order to keep foreign policy out of politics in the campaign. During the 1948 contest, Dulles was Dewey's adviser on foreign affairs and slated to be his Secretary of State. The following year, Dewey appointed him to the Senate to replace the late Robert Wagner, who had resigned.

The campaign which followed was an acid test of bipartisanship which called Truman's bluff. The Democratic President threw the full force of administration influence into an attempt to defeat Dulles and succeeded in electing Lehman as Senator from New York after a struggle marked by characteristic Democratic resort to religious and racial bigotry. For a while Dulles considered waiting in order to run against Lehman again in 1950; then he swallowed his resentment and returned to the State Department as special adviser with special reference to the Far East.

He visited Korea and inspected the Korean defenses on the 38th Parallel a few hours before the Communist sneak attack. Following Truman's decision to intervene in defense of the Korean Republic, Dulles took astute advantage of the changed world situation to negotiate the Japanese peace treaty on terms of mutual reconciliation and respect. London was not enthusiastic, due to British fears of Japanese trade and shipping competition, but Dulles was persistent. He got the treaty and appeased the uneasiness of Australia and New Zealand by negotiating treaties of common defense with those exposed Pacific British dominions. This further exasperated the London government which, like Canada, was already a member of NATO, and argued that Britain should also sit in on the American-Australian-New Zealand alliance. Dulles' visit to London, after Eisenhower's inauguration, was a frosty affair but the moribund European defense treaty took on an appearance of life as a result of his negotiations after he had made it abundantly clear that future American aid was contingent on European co-operation with the public purposes for which the American people taxed themselves to provide that aid.

On the record, John Foster Dulles is, therefore, a man of very considerable attainments, both as a lawyer and as a diplomat.

His career, in turn, reflects his character and background. He is an elder of the Presbyterian Church and a deeply religious man. In 1912 he married the former Janet Avery of Auburn, New York, and has three children and seven grandchildren. His son Avery is training to be a Jesuit priest and nothing in Dulles' long public life angered him so much as Senator Lehman's dishonest charge during the 1949 New York Senatorial campaign that Dulles was a religious bigot.

Dulles used to play golf and tennis when younger; even now, whenever possible, he flies with his wife to camp out in a simple log cabin at his favorite retreat, Duck Island in Lake Ontario. He owns this small island as well as nearby Yorkshire Island, and he and Mrs. Dulles do all their own work on these trips. Although there is no record of his having equalled "Ike's" ability to bake a lemon meringue pie, the Secretary of State is an excellent cook and takes particular pride in his ability to deal rightly with venison. He is also a connoisseur of wine. He is a good bass fisherman and a good shot and an expert sailor. Incidentally, Duck Island may have taught him a useful lesson in caution. At one time there was a sizable herd of buffaloes on his domain, but they have died out, due to their attempts to cross to the mainland in winter before the ice on Lake Ontario was thick enough to hold their weight.

Apart from camping, hunting, sailing, fishing and cooking, his chief diversion is bridge. He plays a sound but rather too deliberate game. He also used to play chess with his brother Allen, but they gave it up by mutual consent when they found that the average game consumed five hours of their crowded time.

Dulles went along with Dewey in supporting Eisenhower but, after consulting with "Ike" and Dewey, refrained from endorsing "Ike" in the pre-convention period in order to work amicably with the Taft supporters on the foreign-policy plank in the 1952 Republican platform. As a former Senate colleague of Taft's, Dulles was careful to keep on friendly terms with "Ike's" rival and he also paid high tribute to General MacArthur, another rival, for his share in the Japanese treaty.

Whatever he may appear in Soviet eyes, Dulles is no warmonger and behind his soft shirt lurks a very astute gentleman. In fact, it is a fair guess that some foreign criticism of his appointment represents annoyance at our having a Secretary of State who really knows international affairs, after the almost unanswerable series of Ed Stettinius, Jimmy Byrnes, George Marshall, and Dean Acheson.

Before his appointment, the chief Republican criticism of Dulles stemmed from the fact that he suggested Alger Hiss, among others, to head the Carnegie Endowment for International Peace, of which Dulles at the time was a trustee. However, Dulles declined to appear as character witness for Hiss after the latter's exposure and was one of the witnesses for the prosecution. On being nominated by Eisenhower, Dulles insisted that the F.B.I. investigate his own loyalty before he sought Senate confirmation. In his necessarily cautious dealings with Senator McCarthy, he began by taking the position that he would not challenge or interfere with the right of Congressional investigation and that he had no time to waste in defending a set of suspect circumstances created by his predecessors. However, he did not hesitate to fight McCarthy's attempt to block the nomination of Charles Bohlen as ambassador to Moscow.

He is a strong, experienced American of Scotch ancestry reaching far back before the Revolution and with a family tradition of distinguished public service. His selection as Secretary of State was almost automatic, once Dewey declined the post. If brains and character can rescue American foreign policy, John Foster Dulles is the man best equipped for the job since President Monroe picked John Quincy Adams to head the State Department after the Napoleonic wars one hundred and thirty-five years ago.

3. THE STATE DEPARTMENT

The reorganization of a huge bureaucratic machine with forty-two thousand employees, packed with the seedy relics of such wartime agencies as O.W.I., B.E.W., and O.S.S. and riddled with scandal, is too big a job for one man. With the Foreign Service, officials can be shifted from post to post, rewarded with ambassadorial responsibility or shipped to Bulawayo, but the department itself is buttressed by civil service and battlemented by loyalty and security requirements which make any change slow and difficult.

Secretary Dulles has made a cautious beginning. With General Walter Bedell Smith as undersecretary and the former head of Quaker Oats, fifty-nine-year-old Donald Lourie of Chicago, to handle administration, the secretary's hands should be free to conduct foreign policy, although it is estimated that in the first three months he had scarcely five minutes of time for that purpose. He personally picked Herman Phleger, the eminent California international lawyer with extensive practice in the Pacific and the Far East, to serve as legal adviser. Former Congressman Thruston Ballard Morton of Kentucky, one of the casualties of the Taft-Eisenhower pre-convention struggle, was selected to handle relations with Congress. Robert Johnson, president of Philadelphia's Temple University, was chosen to take charge of the Voice of America, which had started to crack painfully in the process of changing from an elfin treble to the desired deep bass.

For his own "kitchen cabinet," Dulles picked two young men whom he had known for years and who were deeply loyal to him personally: Carl McCardle and Roderic O'Connor. They are so representative of Dulles' judgment of men that they can be taken as a general report on the spirit of his whole departmental reorganization.

Roderic L. O'Connor comes of a well-to-do Irish Catholic family which has lived in Manhattan for three generations. A slender, fair haired young man of thirty-one, with a large head though a level one, he attended St. Paul's School in Concord, New Hampshire and Yale University, which gave him a law degree in 1947. During the war itself, Rod was a navigator in the Army Air Corps and served in the Mediterranean theater from March of 1943 to October of 1945.

After completing his studies, he was associated with the New York law firm of Kelley, Drye, Newhall, and Maginnes and also made himself active in the New York Young Republican organization. When Dewey appointed Dulles to the Senate, the Young Republicans demanded "recognition" in the form of a job for one of their number as Dulles' assistant in Washington. Since Rod met the specifications, he got the job. He worked in Washington and during the 1949 campaign with Tom Stephens on the political end of Dulles' senatorial career.

After Lehman and Truman had combined to defeat Dulles, Rod went to Germany to do legal work for the Department of Defense in connection with our occupation policies. He returned just in time to follow the Eisenhower campaign, but as a government employee was barred by the Hatch Act from taking an active part. Asked by Dulles to come to work for him again, O'Connor acted as Dulles' detail man in organizing the approach to his State Department duties during the interregnum between election and inauguration day. He accompanied Dulles and Stassen on their quick tour of the West European capitals early in February of 1953. In his State Department job as special assistant, he has as colleague John W. Hanes, Jr. of North Carolina, son of *the* John Hanes who was once Roosevelt's Undersecretary of the Treasury. Young Hanes is also a Yale graduate, class of '49, and also served a three-year stretch in Occupied Germany in the Office of the High Commissioner.

By contrast with this Ivy League duo, Carl Wesley McCardle comes into the State Department by a much longer route. A native of West Virginia, under fifty, McCardle was Washington correspondent of the Philadelphia *Bulletin* at the time when Dulles picked him as Assistant Secretary of State for Public Affairs.

McCardle is tall, dark, large, and excitable, a professional newspaperman whom Dulles met and liked in the course of the various international conferences which McCardle had been assigned to cover for the *Bulletin*.

Like Dulles, McCardle is of Scotch descent with a small-town rural background. His father worked for the telephone company in Morgantown, West Virginia. From the very start, Carl had printer's ink in his blood. After graduating from the local high school, he ran a county weekly paper in Cameron, West Virginia. Then for a year he taught school at Windy Gap where he also served as correspondent for the Moundville *Daily Echo.* He next went to Washington and Jefferson College in Pennsylvania, and also worked at night as reporter for the Washington *Observer.* After that he went on to study law at Temple University in Philadelphia, accompanying his studies by working as copy boy on the *Bulletin.* He received his law degree in 1931 but has never been admitted to practice.

The *Bulletin* promoted him rapidly, to feature writer, to diplomatic correspondent, to Washington correspondent, to European correspondent, finally making him head of its Washington bureau in 1949. In the course of this career, McCardle covered Hitler's seizure of Austria and Czechoslovakia. From 1943 on, he covered most of the major diplomatic conferences: Hot Springs, Atlantic City, San Francisco, the meetings of the Council of Foreign Ministers in Moscow, Paris, London, and New York, and the sessions of the United Nations.

Dulles soon found it useful to take McCardle along on his own special trips and the two were together in Korea just before the Communist attack in June of 1950 and conferred with MacArthur in Tokyo before it was known whether Truman would intervene. They were actually airborne back to America when they received the fateful word that American troops had been ordered into action in Korea. They also traveled together on the various trips required to negotiate the Japanese treaty.

His State Department job brings in a man who has a sense of journalistic statesmanship which is rare in Washington. No Press Club Bar "kingmaker," McCardle is a responsible reporter with a talent for personal friendships. He is no administrator and has the reputation of never being on time for any appointment, but in his present position he is mercifully not required to perform any administrative duties, but rather to hold himself free to work with Dulles on large affairs. He is highly emotional and frequently attacked with political jitters, and has made enemies as well as friends, both in the Washington press corps and in politics.

As with so many of the New Republican leaders, Carl McCardle is essentially a small-town old-stock American. He married at the age of thirty and he and his wife, the former Dorothy Bartlett of Philadelphia, have one child, a daughter.

However, McCardle is much more than a camouflaged super-State Department press officer. Secretary Dulles values his advice on matters of policy quite as much as on the proper wording of a press statement or the drafting of a speech.

4. Envoys Extraordinary

With our European alliance in jeopardy, London, Paris, Rome, and Bonn automatically became the chief political posts for our diplomacy. Career diplomats could be and were assigned to such important centers as Tokyo, Madrid, and Moscow, but the Eisenhower administration decided that in the chief capitals of Western Europe our envoys should represent the moral, material, and intellectual leadership of the New Republican Party.

In point of fact, London had always been the chief political post in American diplomacy. With important economic and currency issues arising between Washington and London, Eisenhower picked as ambassador the greatest institutional banker in the United States, sixty-seven-year-old Winthrop W. Aldrich of the Chase National Bank. The age of the great personal bankers, such as J. P. Morgan and George Baker, had passed with the Banking Act of 1935, much of it the work of Aldrich himself. As chairman of the board of directors of New York's gigantic Chase Bank, he not only possessed a mastery of the financial and monetary elements in Anglo-American relations; he had also backed "Ike's" Presidential candidacy with all his very great influence and experience.

Aldrich was, in fact, almost the last of the "Old Republicans" in that he was born to moderate wealth in Providence, Rhode Island, in 1885. His father, Nelson Aldrich, was a United States Senator for thirty years, the co-author of the famous Payne-Aldrich tariff which wrecked the Taft administration, and the chairman of the National Monetary Commission which foreshadowed the creation of the Federal Reserve system. Yet when Aldrich testified to a Senate committee that his personal fortune was only three hundred thousand dollars, one Democratic Senator refused to believe him and then, convinced of the facts, opposed his nomination to London on the ground that the great banker was too poor to maintain the post.

Up to a certain point, Winthrop Aldrich's career might have been composed by John Marquand. He graduated from Harvard in 1907 and from Harvard Law School in 1910. He entered a private law firm in New York in 1911 and, after a stretch of service on convoy duty with the navy in the first World War, he joined the law firm which served as counsel for the Equitable Trust. With the onset of the panic of 1929, he became president of the Equitable. A year later he merged it with the Chase bank, and became its president, being elected as chairman of its board in 1934, a post he held until "Ike" sent him to London. A former Chase attorney, John McCloy, who had been United States High Commissioner in Germany, chairman of the World Bank and Assistant Secretary of War, then replaced Aldrich at the Chase. The bank is in good hands.

A recital of Aldrich's directorships and public activities, including his many charities, would be tedious. Suf-

fice it to say that Winthrop Aldrich is a personally un-
assuming man who has led a quiet and rewarding life.
Since 1916, he has been married to the former Harriet
Alexander, is the brother-in-law of John D. Rockefeller,
Jr., and is the father of six children, all but one of whom
are living.

The Aldrich family is of old Colonial stock, originally
emigrating from Derbyshire, England and settling in
Massachusetts in 1631. His clear-headed sponsorship of
banking reform after the 1929 panic marked him as "a
traitor to his class" in the sense that it purged high finance
of high-level racketeering, but it also entitles him to
respect as an economic statesman. So obviously was he
"Ike's" choice for London that his nomination leaked to
the press before the State Department could ask the usual
Foreign Office clearance; Anthony Eden and Winston
Churchill were rather miffed to read the news in the
papers before their official sanction had been requested.

To Germany, by contrast, Eisenhower has sent, not a
banker but a chemist, former President James Bryant
Conant of Harvard, to serve as our High Commissioner
and, on ratification of the overdue Germany peace contract, as our ambassador to Bonn. Conant comes of an old
blue-blooded Bay State codfish-and-bean family and recently distinguished himself by his work on the atom
bomb. Following liberal educators such as Eliot and
Lowell, Conant faced a difficult job when he became
president of Harvard in 1933, when only forty years old

and a chemist into the bargain. Before that time he had served as a major in the Chemical Warfare Section of the army in World War I and had returned to teach at Harvard and to study in Germany. His work on hemoglobin and the chemical structure of chlorophyll—which holds the secret of plant growth as well as of sweet breath—gave him world recognition.

Bonn is not his first diplomatic assignment. He negotiated the wartime agreement for exchange of scientific defense information with Great Britain, and he went to Moscow with "Jimmy" Byrnes in 1945 in the vain attempt to persuade the Soviet Government to agree to U.N. control of atomic weapons. At the time, Conant did not know that, partly as a result of his British agreement, Dr. Emil Fuchs had been able to steal all the necessary atomic information for Soviet benefit and so enabled Stalin to roll his own uranium nightmare. There was also a little difficulty before the Senate confirmed Conant in his diplomatic post, because the former president of Harvard had uttered the heresy that Communist beliefs do not necessarily disqualify a college professor for teaching his subject. This lapse from academic grace was mercifully overlooked and Conant is now at Bonn, barely 60, interested, intelligent, and prepared to do his part in knitting Germany to the West, where she belongs. It is scarcely necessary to add that Conant, like other New Republicans has stayed married to the same wife, Grace Thayer Richards, also of old Boston ancestry, since their wedding thirty-two years ago. They have two sons and, when in Boston, inevitably reside on Cambridge's famous Quincy Street.

Another great European post, Rome, is to be the scene of a noble diplomatic experiment: the appointment of Mrs. Clare Boothe Luce as the first American woman ambassador in a city which for over two thousand years has considered woman's place as being—well, certainly not behind a desk in the American chancellery.

The wife of Harry Luce has an almost unique capacity for causing controversy. This is partly because she has, unlike most people, a hard, clear mind, and a clever, tart tongue—in addition to beauty, money, and fame in her own name as a successful playwright. All that is pretty hard for most men and all women to take. Actually, except for a couple of divorces, her own and her present husband's, she comes closer to following the New Republican pattern than does any one of the other three political envoys extraordinary to Western Europe. Her grandfather was a Baptist minister in New England. Her father was a violinist in New York City, where she was born. After his death, she was brought up by a stepfather in Greenwich, Connecticut, and had to make her own way by wit, brains, and charm in a highly competitive social and business world.

She made that way with irritating ease and exasperating success: married and divorced wealthy George T. Brokaw; worked for *Vogue* and *Vanity Fair*, becoming the latter's managing editor in 1933, and an extremely good one, too; wrote three books, not bad ones, and three successful plays, including "The Women." In 1935, she married Harry Luce. She also distinguished herself as a war correspondent, was elected to Congress as one of Connecticut's representatives, and was going places politically.

Then God reminded her of His existence. Her only child, Ann Clare Brokaw, was killed in an automobile accident in 1944. Clare Luce turned, as many hurt souls do turn, to the Catholic Church for consolation and was widely hailed as one of Bishop Fulton Sheen's prize converts. Most people, including Clare, would think that God had something to do with it. In the 1952 campaign she went all out for Eisenhower and was believed to want the job of ambassador to Mexico. But "Ike" decided otherwise and the Eternal City was somewhat startled to learn that a woman—a *woman*—would be the next American ambassador. Rome has dealt with Cleopatra, Messalina, and Lucrezia Borgia, but it is doubtful that anyone like Clare Luce has challenged its social attitude in all the intervening centuries.

It will provide a severe test of all Clare's skill and wisdom to counteract the Latin attitude towards members of her sex, to still the searing Roman gossip, and to escape the mocking malice of Italian society. Perhaps it will work out, perhaps it won't, but if it doesn't it will be the first time in Clare's career that she has failed to master any situation in which she found herself. Still slender, blonde, blue-eyed, and beautiful at 50, she has an ambitious man's mind in a small feminine body. If anybody can pull off her assignment in the Rome of Pius XIII and Alcide de Gasperi, Clare Luce can do it.

5. OPERATIONS

Republican Party politics also raised its lovely head in the selection of two of Secretary Dulles' chief colleagues in operating our foreign policy: Harold E. Stassen and Henry Cabot Lodge.

Stassen was born on a farm in Minnesota's Dakota County in 1907, the son of parents recently emigrated from Central Europe.

He graduated from the University of Minnesota, which also gave him his law degree in 1929. In law school he roomed with Wayne Morse, the future Senator from Oregon. After graduation, Stassen practiced law in his own firm in the Twin Cities, served for a while as a county attorney, and then was elected as Republican reform governor in 1938. There had been a rebellion against the corruption of the Farmer-Labor Party state administration, which had imprudently proposed to raise the tax on iron ore mined in the Mesabi Range, and Stassen won.

He made a good record as governor, being elected for three consecutive two-year terms; he delivered the keynote speech at the Republican National Convention of 1940 in Philadelphia, where he was Wendell Willkie's floor manager. He resigned as governor to join the navy in 1943 and served as flag secretary to Admiral "Bull" Halsey for two years in the Pacific, earning citations for gallantry in battle. After serving on the United States delegation at the San Francisco conference in 1945, Stassen traveled widely in Europe and Russia, wrote the inevitable book, and turned up as a Presidential candidate in the Republican Convention of 1948. In the complicated shuffle which followed Dewey's nomination by that gathering, Stassen received the post of president of the University of Pennsylvania as a sort of academic consolation prize.

A professed liberal in politics, he was again a candidate in 1952, winning delegates in Minnesota and Wisconsin, but almost missed the trolley at Chicago, when Senator Thye swung the Minnesota delegates to Eisenhower before Stassen could make up his mind to release them. However, Stassen immediately came to Eisenhower's support in the campaign and was rewarded after the election by being placed in charge of our foreign-aid operations as Mutual Security Administrator. As such, he accompanied Dulles on their quick "look-see" tours of Western Europe and the Near East.

Happily married and the father of two young children, a boy and a girl, at forty-six Stassen has yet to satisfy the general public that he is more than the intelligent opportunist he often appears. Wayne Morse used to like him but no longer approves of him; however, Morse approves of scarcely any member of the human race these days. Certainly there's more to Stassen than opportunism. He is able, energetic, and has attracted a large personal following in the schools and colleges. He has pitched in and is doing a wholehearted job for "Ike." His, too, is an American story, up from a prairie farm to the presidency of a great university and to high official position, with only his own brains to back him.

Henry Cabot Lodge of Massachusetts, our ambassador to the United Nations council, represents another kind of political debt, a debt of honor.

Lodge lost his Senate seat to young John Kennedy of Boston's emerging "Venetian-blind Irish" after concentrating on "Ike's" pre-convention fight and on "Ike's" Presidential campaign. He had faced sure defeat before "Ike's" nomination and his sponsorship of the victorious general did not save him, although it helped.

He is now in his fifty-first year, the grandson of the famous Senator Henry Cabot Lodge who smashed Woodrow Wilson and the League of Nations after World War I, and is the brother of John Lodge, lawyer and former movie actor who is now the Republican governor of Connecticut. Although the Lodge family goes far back into Massachusetts history, they are relatively new in Boston, where they have been prominent for only a hundred years or so. Cabot, as Lodge is called, graduated from Harvard in 1924, married Emily Sears of the famous Boston Sears family in 1926, worked as correspondent and editorial writer for the Boston *Transcript* and the New York *Herald-Tribune*, and then went into Massachusetts politics.

He is tall, youthful, energetic, pleasant, and equipped with a powerful bass voice. He also has courage and luck. He was elected to the Senate in 1936 but took leave before the end of his term to serve with the first American tank detachment in Libya before the North African landings. He was re-elected to the Senate in 1942 but then resigned and served in the army throughout the North African and European campaigns, being separated from the service in December of 1945. The following year he was again elected to the Senate, where he served until his defeat by Kennedy in 1952.

The selection of Lodge as our representative on the United Nations council signalized Eisenhower's determination to conduct a more vigorous American foreign policy. Lodge is a good political floor-fighter and a good rough-and-tumble political speaker, as one must be in Boston politics. While there was some legitimate criticism of his refusal to shake hands with Soviet delegate Vishinsky, there was none of Lodge's powerful arraignment of Soviet military support of the Communists in the Korean War. For once, it seemed possible that the Russians would no longer have things their own way in hurling vituperative propaganda charges at the U.N.

sessions. It is an assignment made to order for Henry Cabot Lodge and should provide the world with evidence that American diplomats no longer intend to take insolence or insult lying down.

6. INTELLIGENCE, INCORPORATED

Neither envoys, however extraordinary, nor policy operations, however ably conducted, will succeed unless the State Department has accurate knowledge of the real trend of foreign nations and the political intentions and necessities of foreign governments—in short, a reliable intelligence service.

Until now there has been no really good foreign political intelligence service available for the guidance of the American government. It has been a hit-or-miss, feast-or-famine, catch-as-catch-can operation, now bloated by crisis, now deluded by foreign infiltration, and again cramped or throttled by Congressional indifference. Since the war, however, a start has been made on a fairly permanent and dependable basis to remedy this horrifying gap in the organization of our foreign policy.

This organization, the Central Intelligence Agency, grew out of the trials and errors of our wartime intelligence and its recent chief, General Walter Bedell Smith, has been transferred to the position of Undersecretary of State, leaving Foster Dulles' younger brother, Allen, in charge of the C.I.A., while the Luce publications have regurgitated C. D. Jackson to direct the associated psychological strategy work of American foreign policy.

Bedell Smith is an expert dry-fly fisherman and a professional soldier who got into intelligence the hard way: according to the late James Forrestal, Smith, when Ambassador to Russia, assured him that the Soviets could not develop the atom bomb within five years. That was in 1948; a year later Stalin let the uranium pop and Smith returned to America to work out a system to prevent that kind of miscalculation from ever again being committed by any responsible American official.

Fifty-eight years old next October, Bedell Smith was born in Indianapolis and began his long military career as a private in the Indiana National Guard. In World War I, he rose from the ranks to the grade of first lieutenant, serving with the 39th Infantry in France.

He liked the army and the army liked him, so after the armistice of 1918 he stuck with the infantry and slowly worked his way up through various commands until the outbreak of World War II brought him to Washington on the general staff. He served as "Ike's" chief of staff in North Africa and at SHAEF and served in the same position through the invasion of Europe and the conquest of Germany. In February of 1946, President Truman, as ever besotted with the notion of military omnipotence, decided to name him as our ambassador to Russia, where he stayed until March of 1949. On his return to America he served as commander of the 1st Corps Area on Governor's Island until the Korean mess convinced even the Truman administration that it needed better political intelligence. So in October of 1950 Bedell Smith took the oath as director of Central Intelligence, where he remained until his former commander sent him over to State to work with Secretary Dulles.

Smith has a sharp mind which is intolerant of "yes" men and a harsh manner which encourages the average man to want to say "yes." He also has the reputation of being a better second in command than commander in any major operation. With stomach ulcers and the extremely pleasant Nory Cline Smith, of Springfield, Missouri—"The Queen City of the Ozarks"—as his wife, he has seen much of the world and has done very well in it. He turned over to his successor, Allen Dulles, the first really professional secret intelligence service in the history of this country since Lincoln employed the Pinkertons to tell him what went on in the Southern Confederacy.

His successor is, of course, "the other Dulles"—Foster's younger brother Allen—a gay and intelligent man of sixty, with graying hair and moustache and a long experience in diplomacy and intelligence.

Like his brother, Allen W. Dulles was brought up in Watertown, New York, went to Princeton, and eventually entered the famous Sullivan & Cromwell law firm. Before taking to law, that training ground of politicians, he spent ten years in the diplomatic service, which he entered in 1916, serving in Vienna, Switzerland, Berlin, Constantinople, and in the State Department until his resignation in 1926.

As a younger man, he was a fair golfer and an excellent tennis player, winning quite a few respectable tennis tournaments, while he used to break ninety regularly on the links. Today he is subject to exasperating attacks of gout, a hereditary ailment in which he cannot even console himself with the thought that he owes it to high living, since it hits him chiefly as the result of intensive high thinking.

Allen Dulles first burst upon the public eye at the age of eight when—it was 1901—he published a book called *The Boer War*, which ran to four editions. Having listened to arguments between his pro-Boer uncle Lansing and his pro-British grandfather Foster, Allen was violently in favor of the Boers. Among other points, his first published work stressed the poor British marksmanship, alleging that in a target test of lyddite on twenty tethered goats, after half an hour's bombardment there were twenty-one goats, since one had given birth to a kid under fire.

During the Second World War, he naturally joined the O.S.S. and handled our wartime intelligence in Switzerland, isolated in a neutral country surrounded by enemies. Early in 1945, he negotiated with General Wolff for the surrender of the German army in Italy. This caused acute umbrage in Moscow, where Stalin feared, in the teeth of all the evidence, that Roosevelt might follow the policy we should have followed, to hold Central Europe for the West, and almost precipitated a major crisis in allied relations. However, Roosevelt stood firm and it was Truman who was responsible for deferring the German surrender in Italy in an attempt to appease Stalin.

After the war, Allen Dulles returned to his law practice in New York. But politics is like other social diseases—hard to cure—and he helped manage his brother's 1949 campaign for the Senate and was otherwise active in New York Republican circles. However, Korea put a term on both his private law practice and his attempt to return to New York life. He moved down to Washington as Bedell Smith's second in command at Central Intelligence; now that Smith has become Undersecretary of State, Allen Dulles has taken charge of C.I.A. Today, with full backing from Eisenhower and with a free hand —including unvouched funds—to conduct his operations, he is prepared to pit his growing organization against the experts of the Old World: France's perennial Deuxième Bureau, the legendary British Secret Intelligence, and the astonishingly successful Russian blend of Soviet espionage and Communist party organization.

The final element in this mobilization of brain power in the service of our foreign policy is provided by C. D. Jackson, the fifty-year old New York City boy who grew up to be publisher of Harry Luce's *Fortune*. Like both the Dulleses, Jackson is a Princeton graduate; he worked with Allen Dulles and Lucius Clay in the postwar period in organizing Radio Free Europe, a program designed to lay the foundations for eventual liberation movements on the shady side of the Iron Curtain.

After a traditional Ivy League education and six years with the family business of importing marble for buildings and tombstones, "C. D."—the initials stand for Charles Douglas—became a career Luce executive, rising to the post of *Life* general manager in 1937. On the outbreak of World War II, he left the Luce outfit and joined the State Department, serving first in Turkey. In 1943, he joined "Ike's" command as deputy chief of psychological warfare in North Africa, Sicily, and Italy, and later in SHAEF. He did not hesitate to tell veteran American diplomat "Bob" Murphy, who had forgotten more about Europe than "C. D." ever knew, where to head in, and otherwise endeared himself to all concerned. After helping in the liberation of France and Belgium, Jackson worked with D.P.'s and liberated war prisoners. Bedell Smith insists that the only time "C. D.'s" psychological warfare really worked was when a bale of his pamphlets, dropped from a bomber, failed to open and plummeted to hit and sink a German barge in the Rhine. France, as usual, gave him the ribbon of the Legion of Honor. Few escape it. Then he returned to New York after V-E Day and resumed his place in the Luce works, finally being appointed publisher of *Fortune* in 1949.

When "Ike's" campaign needed more combat psychology and less lovely prose, he called for "C. D." and Jackson came, breathing fire. He ran "Ike's" speech-writing research bureau at the Commodore and did a good job, if you compare the November election returns with "Ike's" political barometer readings in early September.

Now Jackson has been called into action again. Opinions differ widely as to his personality and ability. His superiors speak of him glowingly, as agreeable, supple, obliging, and highly efficient. His competitors and subordinates express themselves in terms which not only glow but smoke: they dislike him intensely and say so in rather unprintable terms. All agree that he is dynamic, resourceful, hard-driving, and full of ideas, a born American business go-getter who is now, fortunately for us all, in the business of getting after the Russians.

Psychological warfare has been defined as the art of getting the other fellow so mad that he can't think straight. C. D. Jackson should be wonderfully successful at this particular game.

V

KNOW-HOW AND HIGH BRASS

1. THE DEFENSE CRISIS

THE cost of our unwise foreign policy of past decades is measured by a defense crisis of extremely serious dimensions. When statesmen fail, soldiers must stand to arms and the people must sacrifice and suffer.

An eighty billion dollar budget; a standing army—including air and navy—of nearly three and a half million men; the expenditure of billions for military assistance to allied nations all over the globe; an ulcer of a Korean War which has cost nearly one hundred and fifty thousand casualties and ties down nearly one-third of our army; the continuation of military conscription in time of peace, not to mention the development of an internal police organization for security against foreign agents or the unpredictable demands of civil defense: all these represent only the first installment of the price the American people must pay for three generations of idealistic ignorance in foreign affairs.

The mere list of our formal defensive commitments reveals that the messianic impulses of this country since the time of the Boxer Rebellion have made war almost anywhere in the world a war against the United States. With only seven per cent of the world's population we have undertaken the following:

Since 1823, by the Monroe Doctrine, we are committed to defend the countries of Latin America against transoceanic attack. Franklin Roosevelt, in his 1940 speech at Kingston, Ontario, extended this principle to oblige us also to defend Canada.

Since 1922, we have been bound in a treaty of mutual guarantee with the principal Pacific powers.

Since 1931, under the Stimson Doctrine, we stand pledged to refuse to recognize territorial or political changes brought about by force or by the threat of force.

The events of 1917–18 and 1941–45 show that we feel bound in fact to defend Great Britain and Western Europe against conquest without any formal written treaty of alliance.

The United Nations charter of 1945 embodies an obligation to defend all U.N. members against foreign aggression; our intervention in Korea was undertaken in the name of this pledge.

The Rio de Janeiro Treaty of 1947 for hemisphere defense calls for assistance to any American state subjected to an armed attack.

The Truman Doctrine of 1947 commits us to defend

all friendly nations, starting with Greece and Turkey, against either external or internal Communist aggression.

The North Atlantic Treaty Organization of 1949 obliges us to defend the countries of Western Europe against attack.

The Japanese-American treaty of 1951 provides for the use of American troops to defend Japan from foreign attack and to maintain internal order.

The Philippine-American treaty of 1951 commits us to defend the Philippines Republic.

Similar treaties with Australia and New Zealand in 1951 commit us to the common defense of our respective territories in the Pacific.

Since 1951, under NATO, we have undertaken to promote a common army for the defense of Western Europe, including the West German Republic.

We have also proposed, in one form or another, undertakings to protect Iran, to link the Arab countries in defense of the Near East, and a Far Eastern "PATO"— Pacific Area Treaty Organization—which will group the "free nations" of Asia in a common defense with our military support.

We have supported the French in Indo-China and the British in Malaya in their guerrilla war with Communist bandits.

These are rather spacious commitments by a single nation, however productive its industries and however competent its military leadership. Yet the first challenge to them following Acheson's political blunder in announcing that we would not defend Korea—the North Korean attack across the 38th Parallel in June of 1950—came close to producing a major military disaster and eventuated in a costly political and military stalemate which has undermined our prestige throughout Asia.

Only a nation with the illusion of omnipotence could have undertaken such vast responsibilities. The probable cause in our case was the belief that the atom bomb was an American military monopoly, which it never was. A similar contributing cause was the theory that the atom bomb was a sovereign military weapon, which it could never be so long as its only appropriate targets were large industrial cities or closely massed troops.

What makes the defense crisis at Washington even more appalling is the fact that the atom and the hydrogen bombs, which could be terribly effective against our own industrial communities, are only part of the new armory of modern warfare. We must now consider the possibility that our enemy may attack us with biological warfare—attacks on human, plant, and animal life by plague, viruses, and other microorganisms; chemical warfare with its range of elaborately indiscriminate weapons; and propaganda warfare, with its ability to infiltrate our politics and sensitive areas with dissension, sabotage, and treason.

The New Republican team which has come to Washington in an attempt to deal with the resulting defense crisis is composed of unusually competent men. They represent the best brains of our industrial management, one field in which we really lead the world.

So far as procurement, production, and conventional strategy are concerned, the Pentagon is now staffed with the best brains in the country. The associated task of propaganda, intelligence, and political planning lies outside their field and is still the weakest link in our armor. Yet unless the propagandists and the statesmen succeed, the task before the production men and the generals may prove nearly insuperable.

There is not much time left. Our plans for a European defense community under SHAPE have faltered and may prove unrealistic.

Asia itself is either Communist or neutral, except in Malaya and Indo-China where the British and French continue at heavy cost to defend Southeast Asia against Communist revolutionaries.

Africa is beginning to shake under the double earthquake of Arab nationalism in the north and bitter racial conflict in the south, both spurred by Moscow.

South America, which has been taken for granted, has begun to install anti-American governments: some Fascistic, as in the Argentine, others, near the Panama Canal, Communistic.

Our quest for political allies who will share the burden of free-world defense is hindered by widespread resentment against our power, envy of our wealth, and distrust of our motives and of the steadfastness of our policy. If the know-how boys and the Big Brass in the Pentagon are not careful they may wake up some morning and discover that America has allowed itself to be depleted economically and discredited politically to the point of isolation, and that "Fortress America"—that concept of a continental Gibraltar astride the world's great oceans— has become a desperate necessity rather than a dangerous and defeatist dream.

2. GENERAL MOTORS

Defense is the biggest business in the United States. With appropriations running at the rate of fifty billion dollars a year, with three and a half million men and women in the armed forces and nearly a million and a half civilian employees, the Department of Defense is the costly symbol of our attempt to remedy the cumulative mistakes of years of foreign policy by mobilizing our power in a determination to win back the peace our political statesmen lost or, if the worst comes, to defend our very lives.

The method we have adopted is the one which won us military victory in the two world wars of this century: what a defeated Nazi called our "ruthless war industry." Thanks to the so-called "managerial revolution" and to the Roosevelt-Truman inflation which transferred control of industrial policy from the investors to the manager, the postwar struggle finds our ability to turn out everything from atom bombs to chromatic service ribbons at a gargantuan level of efficiency. However, it is an open question whether the resultant defense mechanism is not too intricate and vulnerable in an age of strategic bombing and sabotage. But our industrial system is what we have to fight with and it was natural that Eisenhower should turn to the largest single defense contractor, the gigantic General Motors Corporation, for the man to be his Secretary of Defense.

Arthur Summerfield, then the Republican national chairman, also gave strong support to the idea that Charles Erwin Wilson of Detroit was the man to handle the big job. Both politically and administratively it made sense to let the best of the "know-how" boys take over the tremendous task of defense procurement.

Unfortunately for this attempt to wed Big Business to Big Brass, the bride slipped on a banana peel coming out the church door and the political honeymoon ended with her hip in a plaster cast when it was learned that Mr. Wilson was reluctant to sell his G.M. stock and pay nearly a third of his personal fortune to the government in capital-gains tax in order to take the position. Liberals who hesitate to give a pint of blood to the Red Cross were scornful of such niggardliness. Both Wilson and some of his chosen assistants felt that such a sacrifice of their private wealth, in addition to loss of income, was unreasonable and, despite the standing law against "conflict of interest," there was much justice in their attitude. Eventually all but one of them—Mr. Robert Sprague of North Adams, Massachusetts, who was unable to sell his stock—took the investor's portfolio purging and are entitled to public respect for their willingness to pay a great price for the right to serve their country.

Wilson is a stocky, heavy-built man of sixty-two, clean shaven, with bristling white hair and a ruddy complexion, who is just about as far removed as possible from the old stereotyped, silk-hatted Wall Street capitalist of Communist legend. He is perhaps the most perfect specimen in captivity of the social process which has transferred control of big business from the bankers to the engineers.

He was born in 1890 in the little country town of Minerva, Ohio of Scotch and German ancestry. His father was the principal of the local public school, where his mother had also taught. When young Charlie was four years old, his father transferred to teaching in Mineral City, where the boy attended the public schools. In 1904, they moved again, this time to Pittsburgh, and, after graduating from high school, the future Secretary of Defense went on to Carnegie Tech., which gave him his electrical engineering degree in 1909.

Wilson then got a job as student apprentice with Westinghouse, working with that important electric company's chief engineer, E. C. Lamme, for ten years. It was at Westinghouse in 1912 that Wilson worked on the first self-starter for automobiles. During the first World War, the company worked on army and navy contracts; in 1919 Wilson joined General Motors. He worked for the G.M. subsidiary, Remy Electric Company at Anderson, Indiana, rising from plant manager to general manager in 1925. Then he headed the merged Delco-Remy Company, developing shock absorbers, electric refrigeration, and similar peaceful products, and managing the company's four plants.

The year when Hoover was elected President, Wilson was made a General Motors vice-president and moved to Detroit, where he remained until "Ike" called him to Washington. He not only assisted the company's expanding operations in the United States and Canada, but, more significantly, undertook to handle G.M.'s labor relations after the bitter sit-down strikes of 1937. On the eve of the second World War he was made executive vice-president and in 1940 became acting president when William Knudsen went to Washington to help Roosevelt organize defense production. The following year, Wilson became president of the whole shebang and as such managed General Motors' impressive share in war production. During the war, his company was responsible for twelve billion dollars' worth of munitions output, including a fourth of all tanks and airplane engines, a half of all machine guns and carbines, two-thirds of all heavy trucks, and three-fourths of all the navy diesel horsepower produced in the entire country.

Wilson also made social history in 1950 when he signed a five-year contract with the C.I.O. United Automotive Workers providing for automatic wage changes to reflect changing costs of living. Incidentally, Wilson, like other New Republicans, has stayed married to the girl who was his bride in 1912, Miss Jessie Ann Curtis of Williamsburg, Pennsylvania, and is the father of six children.

When he hit Washington in the opening days of the new administration, he rubbed Congress and newspapermen the wrong way. He treated the Senate committee which passed on his nomination exactly as he would treat the directors of a smaller corporation with which G.M. had decided to deal. He dodged newspaper interviews. In fact, he has issued orders to his defense subordinates to avoid public speeches, interviews and magazine articles, since he believes that he and they will rise or fall on their record for efficient defense production and that publicity is no substitute for achievement.

There is no doubt that Wilson and his team represent the best brains in American industrial management. They are business managers who have weathered both depression and inflation, have learned to get on with organized labor, have mastered industrial technology and, with chiefly their own brains as capital, have raised the nation's economic output to the highest level in history. The defense job they have undertaken is tremendous. Just one minor part of it: military assistance to our allies by the end of 1952 had already shipped to friendly foreign nations over six million tons of "hardware," including twenty thousand tanks and combat vehicles, twenty thousand pieces of artillery, one and a half million small arms and machine guns, over four hundred naval vessels, and more than three thousand airplanes.

If the mobilization of our industrial skill can save the peace, Wilson and his group are the men to do it. Washington has already begun to whisper that "Wilson won't last," that he'll give up after a couple of years and go back to Detroit. But the question of his political popularity is secondary to the test of his ability. Lincoln's Secretary of War, Edwin Stanton, was one of the most disagreeable men in our public life, but he supplied and managed the Federal armies which won the Civil War and has gone down in history as one of the greatest political administrators this country has ever produced. It is a fair guess that Wilson won't leave Washington unless Wilson fails to do his job and so far Charley Wilson has never failed in any production job he has undertaken.

3. — & Company

The members of Wilson's Defense Department team were selected by him personally to help him do his job. They will be judged by their chief's record in office and so cannot be regarded as key political appointments in the Eisenhower administration. But they are all representative of the New Republican movement in terms of industrial management. None of them was originally born to wealth, all of them have succeeded in the intense competition of corporate management. In terms of industry, they are the personal and moral equivalent of such political leaders as Dewey and Duff.

Take Wilson's trouble-shooter, Deputy Secretary of Defense Roger M. Kyes. Kyes is still in his middle forties, a slender, smiling, keen-eyed man. He was born in East Palestine, Ohio, went to Culver Military Academy and then to Harvard Business School, from which he graduated in 1928. He stepped out with his diploma just in time to step into the depression. For the next twenty years, Kyes worked with a variety of concerns, manufacturing aircraft and plows among other products. He joined the General Motors staff in 1948 and two years later became general manager. He married a girl from Harding's home town, Marion, Ohio, and is the father of four daughters.

Or take Harold E. Talbott, "Ike's" Secretary of the Air Force. Talbott is a tall, handsome, determined business executive who was born of well-to-do parents in Dayton, Ohio, sixty-five years ago, and who graduated from Yale in 1911, when the Elis were still winning football games and so had no doubts about anything under the sun. For the next few years he worked with the family business in Dayton on hydroelectric development and construction. As early as 1916, he became interested in aviation when his father and Charles Kettering organized the Dayton Wright Company, one of the few United States airplane concerns which really made planes, both trainers and DeHaviland fighters, during World War I. Talbott served in that war as a major in the Army Air Force. He got his G.M. baptism in 1919 when Dayton Wright was merged into General Motors, and he stayed on until 1925, when he joined Chrysler and moved on to New York. He later was chairman of North American Aviation, and director of Electric-Autolite and of other companies. The same year he moved to New York, he married Miss Margaret Thayer of Philadelphia, and they have four children. Unlike Wilson, Talbott had money behind him from the start of his career but, like his chief, he has gone ahead under his own steam to become a conspicuously successful industrial manager.

Cast in somewhat the same mold as Talbott is Wilson's Secretary of the Army, Robert T. Stevens. He was born in Fanwood, New Jersey, just before the turn of the century, graduated from Yale in 1921, married two years later and is the father of five children. In the first World War, like many other Yale men, Stevens served in the Field Artillery; in the second World War, he was with the Quartermaster Corps, serving in Washington and in Europe and ending up with the rank of colonel. Between the wars he had worked under the N.R.A. Blue Eagle of old Hugh Johnson in and on various business-government advisory groups. He was also chairman of the family textile business and on the directorates of General

Electric, General Foods, Pan American Airways and other business and charitable enterprises. He is a Presbyterian and a member of the Yale Corporation.

Consider, by contrast, Robert B. Anderson of Texas, Secretary of the Navy. He was the only member of the team who did not have to amputate his financial hump in order to pass through the needle's eye of the Senate committee. Anderson was born in Burleson, Texas, forty-two years ago. He went to Weatherford College in Texas, studied law at Texas University, practiced law in Houston, Texas, married a Texas girl, and has two Texas sons. He is a Methodist, a lawyer, and a successful oil operator. He has also served in the Texas state legislature, has been the Lone Star state's assistant attorney general and has held posts on other state agencies, including the post of tax commissioner, boxing commissioner, executive director of the Texas Unemployment Commission, as well as on the Texas Federal Reserve Bank. In recent years he has also managed the famous Waggner Ranch near Vernon, Texas.

The same pattern is repeated in the "Little Cabinet" levels of Defense. Assistant Secretary of Defense John Hannah is just turned fifty, is an expert on poultry, former President of Michigan State College and a native of Grand Rapids, where the furniture comes from. J. F. Floberg, the Assistant Navy Secretary for Air, is a thirty-eight-year-old native of Chicago, a practicing lawyer with four years of active naval service in World War II, including the Tunisian and Sicilian campaigns and at the Salerno landing. Blond, alert, Comptroller Wilfred James McNeil, with the title of Assistant Secretary of Defense, is a native of Boone, Iowa. Now fifty-two years old, McNeil was brought into the Defense Department by the late James Forrestal, after business experience in banking, selling automobiles, and newspaper circulation. Another Forrestal holdover is a dark-haired, serious, bespectacled young lawyer from Saranac, New York, Assistant Defense Secretary Frank C. Nash.

Whatever else such men may be, no one can accuse them of being bloated capitalists or of owing their position to corporate favors or to political favoritism. They are surprisingly young for their achievements and they all achieved their standing by intelligence and by their ability to adjust themselves and the enterprises with which they have been connected to the changing conditions of American business and the shifting pressures of American society. On their ability to help America as a whole to adjust itself to the changing character of defense in a world which itself is in process of violent social and economic upheaval may depend far more than the profits of private business.

Our very hides are at stake, and so Eisenhower has turned instinctively to men much like himself in character and background to undertake the huge task of supplying the munitions needed to defend the Free World.

4. The Big Brass

The armed forces of the United States are unusual among those of the great powers in that we have never possessed a privileged or hereditary officer class. The British navy alone employs the same principle as ours in the selection and training of its commanders, but even in Britain, as in France and Germany, the traditions of feudal nobility have tended to limit high rank to the younger sons of old titled or landowning families. In Russia and other totalitarian countries, there is powerful political party control over the selection and training and, above all, in the promotion or liquidation of military commanders.

The regular armed forces of the United States, almost from the birth of the Republic, have been officered and led by men who were picked on a deliberately representative basis. There have been promotions from the ranks and transfers from National Guard or R.O.T.C. units, especially in time of war; graduates of such military schools as the Virginia Military Institute have held high command, notably George C. Marshall, who rose to be Chief of Staff and a five-star general in World War II. But on the whole, the army, the navy and the air force of the United States are officered by graduates of the United States Military Academy at West Point and the Naval Academy at Annapolis.

West Point has been training the leaders of our army

since 1802; Annapolis has been training our naval officers since 1845. So far, no amount of political pressure or social privilege has enabled a man to enter or graduate from either of these institutions unless he can meet rigorous physical and intellectual requirements. With a few exceptions, appointment to either academy is on the recommendation of a Senator or Congressman. Each member of Congress has the right, subject to examination of the applicant, to appoint an average of one West Point cadet a year. Additional cadets are appointed by the President and the Vice-President, and about forty-five a year can be transferred from the ranks of the enlisted men in the regular army, on the recommendation of the Secretary of the Army. A similar system applies to the appointment of midshipmen to Annapolis.

This method of recruiting our professional army and navy officers insures that there shall be the widest possible geographical representation among the commanders and that no one dominant, social, political, or regional group shall have a monopoly of selecting the officers for our defense forces. High standards of professional training and personal conduct at both academies automatically weed out any unqualified individual who might manage to slip in through political connivance. From the moment of their appointment, they are clothed, fed and paid—miserably paid—by the government, and do not need to possess private incomes to support their rank, as with such British army regiments as the Coldstream Guards.

As a result of this unique representative method of providing the necessary military and naval leadership, the armed forces of the United States today are staffed from top to bottom by men who are the counterpart of the New Republicans who elected Eisenhower and the leaders of the "managerial revolution" whom "Ike" has called in to organize our defense production. Scratch a Sherman Adams or an Omar Bradley, a Charley Wilson or an Admiral Radford, and they are all the same breed of Americans: wholesome, small-town, ambitious types who have climbed to the top of their particular tree, against stiff competition, by their own ability to manage men and deal with critical situations.

The acid test of war, superimposed on this selective process, has brought an exceptionally strong group of leaders to high military command. In fact, the chief criticism which can be made of them is that they are too strong for a weak President or Defense Secretary to manage. Former Defense Secretary Lovett significantly wrote President Truman in December of 1952 of the growing need to make it legally clear under the National Defense Act that the Joint Chiefs of Staff are subordinate to the civil authority of the Secretary of Defense. There have been muttered complaints that the former Joint Chiefs, especially their chairman, General Omar Bradley, decided national policy in foreign relations; there was also reason to believe that the "High Brass" in the Pentagon opposed "Ike's" election because it would place in the White House a President who knew a great deal more about defense than they did.

The truth of the matter is that, under Truman, the Joint Chiefs of Staff ran away with the Defense Department. After V-J Day, the three services faced the grim prospect of a return to lower rank and much lower appropriations. The result was a very human and indecorous scramble for Congressional preference: the air force with its strategic bombers and the atom bomb, the navy with its super-carriers and submarines, the army with its massive organization, personnel, and overseas bases.

Forrestal struggled for unification but it was unification upward, much as Truman's price stabilization stabilized prices upward. What the services did, in effect, was to add all their demands together and send the combined bill to Congress. The situation became so alarming that in 1949, the unification law was amended in order to appoint Omar Bradley as chairman, or moderator, of the three competing services. For a while Defense Secretary Louis Johnson made a determined effort to cut back the service demands, with their competitive stockpiling of material and manpower, but this effort ended tragically when Dean Acheson's State Department boobytrapped the defense establishment into the Korean War.

This unpremeditated commitment had the effect of reopening the Pentagon's *Via Triumphalis* into the United States Treasury and was utilized to resolve service rivalries on the costly but convenient plane of giving the army, navy and air forces whatever they wanted. Service opposition to Eisenhower's election reflected the fear that he would either favor the army against air and navy or, worse still, that he would compel them all to work together as a team and allocate funds to them on the basis of real knowledge of their needs and importance. With Truman they had always been sure of a respectful hearing; with "Ike" things might not be so easy, since he knew more about defense than they did themselves. In fact, the 1952 election almost proved the paradox that the only way to maintain civilian authority over the military is to choose a military man as President.

The former Joint Chiefs were, of course, subject to replacement by the normal processes of their respective services after nomination by the President and Senate confirmation, and all of the Truman group were changed for cause after Eisenhower's first hundred days. The men whom "Ike" found waiting his orders on January 20th, 1953 are, therefore, only indicative of the kind of commanders we have developed in our armed forces.

During the period when they controlled our defense establishment, its costs increased and its quality declined. Men like Ozarks-born, five-star General Omar N. Bradley, Chairman of the Joint Chiefs of Staff; General J. Lawton Collins, Army Chief of Staff; Admiral William Morrow Fechteler, Chief of Naval Operations; and General Hoyt S. Vandenberg, Chief of Staff of the Air Force, are competent and experienced combat commanders. When they dealt with an adoring little civilian who always signed on the dotted lines, they administered chaos and called it defense.

They were not responsible for the original Korean blunder, but they were responsible for the failure to have a good military fire brigade, so to speak, on hand in Japan to deal with that or any other blaze. Their struggles to obtain control of such political functions of defense as central intelligence—first by the air force and then by the navy on a sort of rotation system—reduced the C.I.A. to such a level that all our agents in Eastern Europe were arrested by the Russians. It took Bedell Smith nearly four years to straighten out our intelligence services after they had been the football of the inter-service rivalry of the Joint Chiefs of Staff.

This disastrous record was partly due to the novelty of realistic peacetime intelligence work, but mostly to the traditional political illiteracy of the military mind.

This recurring blindspot toward the political factor in defense is the greatest single weakness in the American military establishment. During the postwar jockeying for advantage between the three services, control of intelligence was sought, not so much to improve the quality and timeliness of the information on which policy decisions are made as to keep it out of the hands of the other services and, above all, to filter the flow of facts to the President of the United States. In much the same way, the Voice of America program directed by the State Department appeared better calculated to impress Congress with its value, for departmental appropriations, than to conduct an effective American foreign propaganda.

Political illiteracy in the army, in particular, was so strongly entrenched that not even repeated organized riots in Communist prison camps in Korea produced a clear and scientific approach to the well-organized Communist political offensive in the camps. And when our truce negotiators met with the Communist representatives to discuss the "cease-fire," they were sitting ducks for the highly trained Communist propagandists, from the moment our representatives appeared under a flag of truce and were photographed as if in the act of surrender to the Reds. Our military men have been schooled to keep out of domestic politics; as a result they are seriously handicapped in dealing with enemies who use politics and propaganda as part of modern armaments.

The best that can be said is that, through politico-military bungling in Europe as well as Asia, some of our commanders are getting an intensive postgraduate education in this important branch of international conflict.

Among the rising group of American commanders, as a result, are now some men who have learned that it is as important to know why nations go to war as it is to know what weapons they possess. They include such officers as General Alfred M. Gruenther, the alert, scholarly fifty-four-year-old newly appointed successor to Ridgway at SHAPE, regarded as the ablest strategist in the army; our present 8th Army commander in Korea, Lieutenant-General Maxwell D. Taylor, who would bear the brunt of any future outbreak of hostilities in that tragic peninsula; his opposite number in Germany, General Thomas Troy Handy, in command of our troops between the Red army and the Rhine; and the tall, dark, saturnine commander of our Pacific Fleet, Admiral Arthur William Radford, promoted to the position of Chairman of the Joint Chiefs of Staff after undertaking the thankless task of protecting Red China against attack from Formosa.

These men who guard our ramparts from the Great Wall of Korea to the Watch on the Elbe are only representative of hundreds and thousands of army, navy and air force officers on whose skill, courage, and judgment the nation may at any time depend for its survival. Despite the baffling combination of massive intelligence and startling stupidity which seems to characterize the military mind in every country, these are also the best we have. They are not a class set apart from the rest of the country, except by their record of service: they are bone and sinew of the same deep-lying social forces—represented by small-town, middle-income, taxpaying neighborly churchgoing families—which have built our nation, created its industries, and now have rallied to the support of Eisenhower and the New Republican Party.

If they can only learn in time that, as the deadliness and

range of weapons increase, military policy becomes increasingly political, then their ordeals in the cold-war period will prove to be an invaluable investment in national security. In the meantime, it is significant that "Ike" sacked the whole lot of high commanders who resented a cut in defense appropriations and opposed the reorganization of the Defense Department, and replaced them with more dependable servants of the civilian government which has trained and paid them to serve the nation as a whole: Ridgway, Carney, and Twining under Radford.

VI

DEEP IN THE HEART OF TAXES

1. "The Silly Old Dollar Sign"

BEFORE 1913, this country lacked the means to finance a major war. This defect in twentieth-century statesmanship was remedied in the nick of time by the creation of the Federal Reserve System and the passage of the income-tax amendment on the eve of World War I. Thanks to these two monumental archways leading to the savings and earnings of the American people, in that conflict we were able to put five million men in uniform, suffer three hundred and fifty thousand casualties, and raise the national debt from a bare one billion dollars in 1915 to more than twenty-five billion dollars in 1919.

Before 1935, this country again lacked the means to finance a total war. This defect in the age of Hitler and Stalin was also remedied just in time by the devaluation of the dollar and by the system of social security payroll deductions which paved the way for the payroll withholding tax of World War II. Thanks to inflation and to the check-off on salaries and wages, in this second conflict we were able to put over fifteen million citizens in uniform, suffered over one million casualties, and raised the national debt from forty-nine billion dollars in 1941 to almost two hundred and seventy billion in 1946.

This latter achievement was due to the fiscal policies of President Franklin Delano Roosevelt. With much the same patrician impatience which had led a British prime minister to refer to decimal points as "those damned dots," President Roosevelt, in launching Lend-Lease in 1941, proclaimed his intention to get rid of "the silly old dollar sign" in our aid to the nations which were fighting the Rome-Berlin Axis. Over that once sacred dollar sign he had exercised his fiscal *droit de seigneur* for the eight years of the New Deal, using the devaluation of the dollar and other inflationary measures to increase the national debt from seventeen billions under Hoover to nearly three times as much by the time of Pearl Harbor.

For the price of poor statesmanship is debt and taxes. Yet in spite of orthodox sneers at the New Deal's inflationary and spending policies, it is fair to assert that they helped the United States avoid industrial fascism after the banking crisis of the early 1930's. Historically, fascism has attacked industrial nations whose capital has been destroyed by inflation or war. This loss of funds compels industries to create their own capital under forced draft, out of high prices and low wages, a combination which requires special police and political authority. The Milan industrialists were behind Mussolini, just as the Ruhr magnates were behind Hitler. Roosevelt's seizure of the banks, and his programs for public works, relief, and refinancing private indebtedness made enough capital available in time to head off the ugly drift toward a violent reaction in the steel, coal, and automotive industries.

The cost of this deliverance was the creation of an inflationary mechanism which, as Roosevelt warned, in the hands of weak or corrupt officials could destroy the people's liberties. Roosevelt's warning was aimed at Wall Street, but he would have been wiser to watch Kansas City. After his death, the successors to his administration turned to inflation and deficit spending as the drunkard returns to his bottle and made a permanent policy out of a perilous expedient.

The result was a spiraling price inflation, largely postwar, which cut the value of the dollar by nearly fifty per cent and raised all costs, including the cost of rearmament, depleted all savings, cut all salaries and fell with crushing force on the very middle-income business and professional homes which were the concrete expression of the old American dream. The Federal Reserve Board had been browbeaten by the Treasury Department into an abdication of its duty to regulate the volume of credit and was compelled, instead, to prostitute itself in order to maintain the value of government bonds, as though

you could bring on warm weather by holding a lighted
match under the bulb of a thermometer. By the time this
imitative magic was discontinued in 1951, the damage
had been done; by then the Korean War provided fresh
inflation of wages, prices, savings, and security.

When "Ike" stepped into the White House, here was
the booby trap he found waiting for him as the gift of
his predecessor.

The national debt stood at nearly two hundred and
seventy billion; Mr. Truman had budgeted for a ten billion deficit in 1953; the Republicans stood pledged to
debt reduction and a balanced budget.

Congress had authorized an additional eighty billion
for expenditures by the Federal departments, chiefly on
defense.

Nearly eighty billion of the national debt was due or
callable before the end of 1956, and interest rates were
due to jump by about forty per cent, from 2.35 per cent
to an indicated 3.25 per cent, raising the annual cost of
debt service by perhaps as much as a billion a year.

The tax rates were the highest in America's peacetime
history, ranging from twenty to ninety-two per cent. on
personal incomes. Nearly one-third of the national income of three hundred billion depreciated dollars went
to pay the cost of government, with the Treasury taking
twenty five billion from pay envelopes, thirty six billion
from income and profits taxes, ten billion from other
excise and luxury taxes—for a total of seventy billion. In

addition to all this was the cost of state and local government.

The Republicans had promised to economize on this terrifying Federal budget but barely a sixth of the whole eighty billion went for the normal costs of the national government: fifty five billion was for defense and foreign aid, eleven billion for interest and the veterans. It was clearly impossible to keep the party's promise to balance the budget and reduce the taxes unless there was to be a major default on the basic commitments the American Government had already made at home and abroad. The silly old dollar sign had come home to roost and it looked like a hungry vulture.

It was under these unpromising conditions that Eisenhower's new Secretary of the Treasury, George M. Humphrey of Cleveland, Ohio, announced the following program for fiscal management:

"... first, that we will have a sound and stable dollar, not one of declining value; second, that we do not spend more than we earn; third, that we pay a little down on our debts from time to time instead of rapidly borrowing more; fourth, that we keep our credit good by properly managing the debts we already have; fifth, that slowly but surely and definitely we reduce the too heavy burden of taxes which, buried in the cost of everything we buy, are stifling initiative and increasing the cost of living; sixth, that we maintain free markets in which the great American consumer can buy what he needs when he wants it and choose for himself what he will buy at prices he is willing to pay; seventh, that producers are free to strive to produce more, better and cheaper goods to compete for the consumer's favor in buying their particular products in competition with everything else; eighth, that we protect the savings of the old, their insurance and their pensions; ninth, and above all, that we preserve for the young the great symbol of America, the opportunity to advance and improve themselves to the limit of their own abilities and their own hard work and endeavors."

2. GOLIATH OF THE GOITER BELT

In the telecast in which Secretary Humphrey delivered this admirable description of what it would be like to live in a really free economy, Columbia Broadcasting's political impresario, Mr. Eric Severeid, described George Humphrey as "a first-class example of the managerial revolution which has produced a fresh new type of restless, imaginative business managers who see property as fluid, changing, expanding, in an inseparable working relationship with the government and the whole expanding society."

Humphrey himself had never expected to enter the cabinet and his selection, as a known Taft supporter, was made by Eisenhower without the knowledge of Senator Taft. A flexible-minded, highly successful banking and industrial statesman, Humphrey is generally regarded as not only the greatest business leader in Cleveland, Ohio but also as the ablest man in the Eisenhower cabinet. When the unsought treasury post was offered him, he promptly disposed of all investments which could constitute a "conflict of interest" with his official duties and accepted the gargantuan task of cleaning up the scandal-ridden and demoralized Treasury Department he had inherited from Mr. Truman's crony, John Snyder. In this course, Humphrey was true, not only to his own character and career, but to the high civic tradition of Cleveland, where he had made his home for more than thirty-five years. Whether because of the almost constant overcast of clouds from Lake Erie or because of the absence of iodine in the drinking water which places that city in the heart of the famous "goiter belt," Clevelanders are acutely interested in politics and are vigorous partisans from the cradle. Since the days of Tom Johnson and Newton Baker, Cleveland has shared with Houston, Texas the distinction of being the most political-minded city in the United States. It is also, of course, one of the most vital industrial communities in North America.

Humphrey is a Clevelander only by adoption. He was born in the small Michigan town of Cheboygan sixty-three years ago. His parents were only moderately well-to-do and he had to make his own way. He was brought up in the bustling little city of Saginaw, Michigan, where he attended the public schools and played on the Saginaw High School football team, helping it win the state championship in 1907. After this he went on to the State University at Ann Arbor, where he joined Psi U and graduated with a law degree in 1912. As soon as he had passed his state bar exams, he returned to Saginaw, joined his father's law firm, and married a Saginaw girl named Pamela Stark.

Five years later, as a result of his legal attainments, he was offered the position of general counsel of old Mark Hanna's famous M. A. Hanna & Co. in Cleveland, where he remained until 1953, rising gradually to the rank of partner, vice-president, executive vice-president and finally, in 1929, president of the whole concern, becoming at last its chairman of the board of directors in 1952.

George Humphrey possesses much more than a clear legal brain. He has an easy, adaptable personality and is a thinker. It is a tribute to his wisdom that, although the Hanna Company deals primarily with such controversial products as coal and steel, not once during all the labor turmoil of the last twenty years and more of this corporate leadership has his company been involved in conflict or unfavorable public prominence. Mark Hanna was long regarded as a symbol of silk-hatted conservatism; it is often forgotten that he pioneered in decent labor relations and that the concern he founded has kept its name and its nose clean, labor-wise, tax-wise and government-wise.

At a time when other coal and iron masters were losing money or hiring finks and thugs to police their workers, under Humphrey—even during the depression—the Hanna business not only earned a profit but expanded. In association with the National City Bank of Cleveland, of which he is a director, the company proceeded to combine Weirton Steel, Great Lakes Steel and the Hanna interests in iron mines, lake shipping, and blast furnaces to form the remarkably successful National Steel Corporation in the very year of the 1929 panic.

The year which saw the end of World War II also witnessed Humphrey's comparable achievement in organizing Pittsburgh Consolidation Coal Company, a merger of the Pittsburgh and the Consolidation Coal Companies, to form the largest bituminous coal-producing corporation in the world.

And the year which witnessed the Communist attack in Korea saw Humphrey organize the Iron Ore Company of Canada to develop the huge newly mapped iron deposits in Labrador and Quebec. With the fabulous Mesabi range depleted of its ore by two world wars, these new reserves guarantee the future of the Great Lakes steel industry in North America. In this connection, where twenty years ago they damned it as "a socialistic ditch," there is no doubt that the Hanna Company and its banking associates now applaud the decision of the Canadian government to develop the St. Lawrence Seaway and thus permit the Labrador ore to move to the blast furnaces of National Steel on the lower lakes.

It is in achievements like these that Secretary Humphrey takes legitimate pride. They were managed without fanfare or scandal and typify business foresight and industrial imagination at their best. The same foresight also brought him into the Committee for Economic Development and he is one of the trustees of that remarkable mobilization of America's managerial brains for public service. He has also been active in other industries, including rayon, copper, and sugar. At one time he was chairman of the Department of Commerce's Business Advisory Council and also served on the E.C.A. advisory committee which reconsidered Roosevelt's hasty plan to dismantle the German factories and turn their machinery over to Russia. A list of the other business, educational, and charitable organizations with which Humphrey is connected reads like an institutional *Who's Who:* Academy of Political Science, Tax Foundation, Iron and Steel Institute, United States Council of the International Chamber of Commerce, Harvard Graduate Business School, Ford Foundation, and Massachusetts Institute of Technology, as well as hospitals and medical schools.

Thus George Humphrey brings into the Eisenhower administration a broad, fresh, and practical conception of wealth, not as measured in terms of dollar profits, but in terms of production, employment, and utilization. He is a leader of the new business philosophy which realizes that the purpose of industry is not to produce wages for workers, profits for investors or tax revenues for Washington, but that all these necessary things can come only if industry's chief function is to produce needed goods and services at a price people can afford to pay. This view cuts squarely across the old-fashioned economic sentimentalities of the past. It challenges the creed of organized labor that business exists primarily to provide jobs for union members; it abandons the traditional banking view that industry should concentrate on net profits and dividends; and, judging by his published statements, it is in conflict with the bureaucratic concept of industry as a convenient mechanism for collecting taxes from the community and turning them over to the government.

So George M. Humphrey is the man who, if anyone can, will take us back to the original nature of American economics: a free market, private initiative, incentive for risk, and rewards proportionate to effort, judgment, and success. This was the prevailing economic climate of the 1890's when he was a small boy in Michigan and William McKinley was in the White House. Tempered by the strains and responsibilities of the past fifty years, these ideals still hold the secret of our tremendous industrial growth, a growth of productivity so fantastic that not even the fiscal aberrations of twenty years of lethal taxation have yet demoralized our industrial system or debased our currency beyond repair. Humphrey and men like him have, in fact, been giving the dollar its real value, in terms of coal, steel, processing, and transportation, without reference to whether gold sells for thirty-five dollars an ounce or whether we have twenty-three billion dollars buried in Fort Knox. Such trifles are only the symbols for the real values represented by the things people eat, use, and wear. That is the basic philosophy of the man whom "Ike" has selected in the effort to help us all return to a freer way of life.

3. "As Fine As You Could Possibly Imagine"

To help him do his job, Humphrey has picked what he publicly called "as fine a group of men as you could possibly imagine." One of them is a woman. All of them have come up, much as Humphrey did, from simple homes and with few initial advantages. They include a former Harvard professor, the daughter of a western miner, a statistician from Virginia, a Georgia lawyer who was born in California, a Cleveland lawyer, and a New York camera manufacturer who was born in Georgia. Together, they are a cross section of middle-class American business achievement at its best and most diverse. Individually, each is a story of outstanding personal success, based on ability, hard work, and little or no luck.

There have been rumors that, under Roosevelt, Communists filtered into the Treasury Department. Henry Morgenthau's assistant, the late Harry Dexter White, denied under oath that he was a Communist: a few hours later God struck him dead of heart failure, so he is no longer subject to investigation. He is believed to have originated the fantastic "Morgenthau Plan" to strip Germany of machinery for the benefit of Soviet industry and to leave Europe's workshop a potato patch and cow pasture. He may also have authored the vicious excess profits tax, which in effect decrees that there shall be no new major business enterprises in the United States. Certainly, under Roosevelt's and Truman's administrations, to inherit, give, or earn money was punished as severely as, and more surely than, the average mayhem or manslaughter. Income taxes range up to ninety-two per cent. and start after the first six hundred dollars of personal income; inheritance taxes climb from seven per cent. on a five thousand dollar estate to seventy-seven per cent. on ten million dollars, regardless of the number of heirs. Gift taxes start at 2½ per cent. on five thousand dollars and soar to fifty-seven per cent. on four hundred thousand dollars. Property may not be theft but the New Deal Treasury punished its transfer as a serious civil offense. This may not be orthodox Communism but it strikes at the root of our basic institutions: individual initiative, private charity, and the family.

Certainly no one could say that Humphrey's deputy, W. Randolph Burgess, is a Communist or even a radical, since he was born sixty-four years ago in Newport at a time when it was the center of America's most unregenerate wealth. He was born with a silver spoon, if not in his mouth, at least in his porringer, and enjoyed an extensive education at Brown, McGill, and Columbia universities. A large, bald, excessively shy man, Burgess is today the greatest living expert on United States government bonds and was chairman of the board of the merged City Bank Farmers Trust Company of New York at the time "Ike" called him to help refinance the public debt.

For nearly ten years, Burgess was in charge of the "open-market" operations of the New York Federal Reserve Bank, buying and selling government securities as needed to regulate the supply of bank credit. In 1938, he joined the National City Bank of New York and stayed with them until coming to Washington. The first refinancing he undertook after "Ike's" inaugural—nine billions in February of 1953—clearly indicated that interest rates were rising and that the era of cheap inflationary credit was coming to an end.

The Treasury, of course, is more than a broker for government securities. It is the oldest, best, and most intelligent operating agency of the Federal Government. In tax collection alone, the Internal Revenue Service raked in eighty-three billions in the fiscal year ending June 30th, 1952. That meant that ninety million individual tax returns were handled by about fifty-five thousand officials, some of whom were not entirely honest. The new Commissioner of Internal Revenue is a protégé of Virginia's economy-minded Senator Byrd, a certified public accountant from Richmond, Virginia, who was born about the time Byrd's predecessor, Carter Glass, was getting ready to revise the state constitution so as to disenfranchise the poor. T. Coleman Andrews was born in 1899, when the whole nation had been frightened by Populism and Bryanism. He is surely no radical, but is a practicing accountant who has served both the State of Virginia, the Navy Department, and the General Accounting Office and is recognized as one of the nation's leading statistical authorities. He can be relied upon to root out dishonesty among the collectors of this torrent of taxes.

Another Treasury position which used to be more important than the internal revenue post is that of the Assistant Secretary in charge of Customs, the Coast Guard, and the Lighthouse Service. Before 1913, tariff duties provided the bulk of the Federal revenues. Today they account for a measly half billion dollars, less than one per cent. of the total. The job itself is one which calls for real administrative ability to combat smuggling, maintain air-sea rescue services and ice patrol, inspect merchant vessels, guard against sabotage in ports, tend to thousands of lighthouses and lightships and, in wartime, to integrate the coast guard with the navy. This assistant also supervises the three mints at Philadelphia, San Francisco, and Denver and checks on the purity of the coinage. This post is now held by a forty-six-year-old Cleveland lawyer named Horace Chapman Rose, who studied at Princeton and at Harvard Law School. In 1932 Rose served as one of Supreme Court Justice Oliver Wendell

Holmes' famous series of secretaries—Tom Corcoran was another—before joining a Cleveland law firm. During the war he worked with Bernard Baruch on problems of industrial mobilization and reconversion. After his demobilization he resumed his law practice, with some time out as an economic consultant for Paul Hoffman's E.C.A. operations.

Possibly the most romantic appointment to the least romantic Treasury post is that of Ivy Priest to be Treasurer of the United States. Her job includes processing about three hundred million Government checks a year, keeping track of the twenty-eight billions of dollars of currency in circulation, replacing worn-out bills, and forwarding fresh supplies of coin and paper money to the banks. Her name now goes on all new bills issued by the government and the signature Ivy B. Priest will soon become as well-known as the engraving of Benjamin Franklin.

Mrs. Priest was born in the little mining town of Kimberley, Utah in 1905, the oldest child of a Mormon miner who rejoiced in the name of Orange Decatur Baker. She had graduated from the local public schools and was in her freshman year at the University of Utah when her father fell ill. She immediately abandoned her education and returned home to help take care of the family, including six brothers and sisters. She worked as a telephone operator, she worked as a salesgirl, she studied at night and took correspondence courses. In 1934 she also went into politics as president of the Utah Young Republicans. A year later she married Roy Fletcher Priest and is the mother of three children; her home is in the little town of Bountiful, Utah. Her flair for politics was phenomenal, and by 1944 she became Republican National Committeewoman for Utah, holding the post until this year. During "Ike's" campaign she headed the women's division of the Republican National Committee; her appointment is of course partly a political reward for having done a good political job. But Ivy Priest is more than patronage: she is vigorous, practical, dynamic, interested in civic progress and social welfare. Among other things she is responsible for the first minimum-wage law for working women in Utah.

Like Secretary Humphrey, all of these officials severed all business and professional connections before seeking Senate confirmation. Not one of them has been divorced. All are married, family men, and responsible citizens, who fit perfectly into the middle-income, middle-way pattern which created and supports the Eisenhower administration.

4. Budget-Making and Budget-Breaking

The same is true of George Humphrey's opposite number, across West Executive Avenue from the White House: Budget Director Joseph M. Dodge.

The task which Dodge inherited from hair-trigger

Harry is a dismal one. The Democratic administration, convinced that nothing in the world could not be settled by a big appropriation, countered the uxorious Republican plans to balance the budget by planning for a whopping deficit this year and piling up authorized expenditures, over and above the budget, equal to a single year's Treasury receipts. The first action the new team took was to order a complete freeze on the government departments. No new appointments, no jobs to be filled, except when absolutely indispensable and certified as such. In addition, Dodge issued orders that the employees of the Budget Bureau should promptly report any obstruction or lack of co-operation on the part of other Federal officials. This represents the first honest attempt in twenty years to tighten the purse strings and to use the power of the purse, as originally intended when the Budget Bureau was established, to assert the authority of the White House over the executive departments.

Under Roosevelt, inspired by some Presidential rubbish uttered to justify his taking it under his wing, the Budget Bureau got above itself. During the war years, with the President's unvouchered funds and general grants of authority at its disposal, this purely administrative agency tried from time to time to make public policy rather than see that funds were spent for the purposes already determined. President Truman was no fiscal purist but he called in an old-timer, Frederick J. Lawton, and put him in charge of the Bureau of the Budget. By then, the military establishment was calling the turn and naming the appropriations, and the Bureau merely served as a sort of M.P. directing financial traffic. Lawton, a remarkably warm-hearted, intelligent man to be in such a thankless post, has been kept on in Washington assisting "Ike's" chosen Budget Director and to serve the White House as a pipeline to the past.

If any one official can control self-willed and self-perpetuating bureaucratic machinery, Joseph Morrell Dodge is the man to do it. He was born in Detroit sixty-two years ago, had only a public-school education, and began his business career at the age of sixteen as a bank messenger. By sheer personal ability, he slowly rose in the banking business until, at the time of his appointment by Eisenhower, he had become the president of the oldest financial institution in Michigan, the Detroit Bank. In addition to being a director of Chrysler and several insurance companies, he has also been president of the Michigan Bankers Association, the American Bankers Association, and the Association of Reserve Bankers. He might be described as a banker's ideal of a banker.

Although he has the general facial expression of the man who turns down your loan application at your local bank, he has a record of numerous civic and charitable activities, including the Michigan Cancer Foundation, the Detroit Symphony Orchestra, the American Cancer Society, the Greater Detroit Hospital Fund, and the local Detroit chapter of the Foundation for Infantile Paralysis.

Dodge met "Ike" during the war after he came to Washington for the Army Services Forces and the War Contracts Board in 1941. Following V-E Day, the War Department sent him over to Frankfurt, Germany to serve as financial adviser to Eisenhower's military government. "Ike" made him director of finance for all the American forces in the European theater and formed a high opinion of his ability and judgment. Truman gave him a Medal of Merit for his work in Germany and in 1950 Dodge also received the Medal for Exceptional Civilian Service for his work on the economic stabilization of Japan.

As a matter of fact, since 1941 Dodge has been more of a government official than a private citizen. After the war he was an American delegate on the Austrian Treaty Commission at Vienna. Later in the same year—this was in 1947—he attended the London meeting of the Council of Foreign Ministers as poor George Marshall's deputy for Austrian affairs. For a four-year period, Dodge was a member of the E.C.A.'s advisory committee on the fiscal and monetary problems involved in foreign aid. For three years, from 1949 to 1952, he also served as American Minister and financial adviser to the Supreme Commander of the Allied Powers in Japan, making four trips to that country, and in 1952 he worked with Acheson and Dulles as a consultant on economic and financial matters affecting Japan. In his spare time, if any, he also acted as financial consultant to the Department of the Army.

When Truman creditably broke partisan precedent and offered his full co-operation to the incoming Eisenhower administration in advance of the inaugural, "Ike" promptly named Dodge and sent him to the White House to consult on budgetary and fiscal matters. Dodge established the first Republican beachhead in the White House, while his colleague, ex-Senator Henry Cabot Lodge, did the same at the State Department.

His associates report that this able and experienced financier in charge of the Budget Bureau is easy to work with, reasonable in his plans, and remarkably ready to listen to reason. Upon his firmness and judgment, no less than on the skill and imagination of George Humphrey and his Treasury associates, depend the solvency and financial integrity of the Eisenhower administration.

The challenge they face is simple and preposterous. The demand for tax reduction, as promised by the 1952 Republican platform, is politically appealing. Canada and England have reduced taxes and Republican Congressmen who face re-election in 1954 are eager to follow suit. If it were only a matter of urging Eisenhower to veto a bill to reduce taxes, there would be little problem. But the task is to persuade Congress to renew onerous taxes which would otherwise automatically expire.

The discriminatory excess-profits tax, which favors large-scale, long-established businesses at the expense of new and smaller enterprises, is due to expire on June 30th, 1953. A special eleven per cent. addition—the Truman addition—to the personal income tax, ordained after the outbreak of the Korean War, is due to expire on December 31st, 1953. If Congress does nothing, the lapse of these two revenue measures will cost the Treasury nearly six billion dollars in revenue. Startling as it seems, the best bet is for a compromise, under which the eleven per cent. Truman annex to the income tax and the excess-profits tax will both expire together on September 30th, 1953. These tax cuts would thus take effect in time for the 1954 elections.

But if they do take effect, what becomes of the balanced budget and what of the national debt limit of two hundred and seventy five billion dollars? With increased interest rates due to add materially to the cost of debt service, and with Mr. Truman's last budget aiming at an eight to ten billion dollar deficit, the Eisenhower administration might easily turn up with a deficit of between ten and fifteen billion dollars in 1954, although the Republicans solemnly promised and vowed to balance the budget and to end deficit financing.

For this is the end of the trail for the Roosevelt-Truman easy-money, "silly old dollar sign" policy. And this is the end of a fiscal insouciance which led F.D.R. to appoint one Secretary of the Treasury because the latter had composed a special inauguration march for him in 1933, and another because he lived near Hyde Park in

Dutchess County, New York and knew something, but not much, about farm credit. It is the end of Kansas City politics in the Treasury, politics which turned over collectorships of internal revenue to deserving and grasping Democrats, and which led Mr. Truman to appoint one Secretary of the Treasury because he needed to be "fattened up" for a Supreme Court appointment and another because he came from the Ozarks. The Republican fiscal team comes from the grass roots of America. Perhaps they, too, need to be shown but for the present they are most likely to be seeing stars, as they try to throttle down the runaway Democratic inflation to a safe and steady pace.

VII

WE CAN DO IT BETTER!

1. THE MORE ABUNDANT LIFE

TWENTY years ago, when Roosevelt became President, the overwhelming majority of Americans were willing to accept, if not wholly approve, his spirited attempt to deal with the scandal of misery in the midst of plenty: fourteen million unemployed, idle factories, closed mines, foreclosed farms, insecurity, hunger, bankruptcy, suicide, and despair in the presence of an abundance of fuel, food, energy, capital, skill, and strength.

The New Deal took its moral imperative from the President's avowal that the mission of his administration was, in New Testament terminology, to establish the more abundant life, especially for that one-third of the nation which was "ill-housed, ill-clad and ill-nourished." A whole generation of young, ardent idealists came forward to help remake America with a semi-revolutionary fervor which was impatient of all financial or legal obstacles.

Less than ten years later, when Roosevelt formally abandoned "Dr. New Deal" in favor of "Dr. Win-the-War," it was beginning to appear that his basic solution for the problem of misery in the midst of plenty was to get rid of the plenty.

A growing scarcity of foods and fibers was deliberately created by buying up "surplus" farm produce and destroying it, impounding it, giving it away to foreign nations; millions of pigs were slaughtered and their meat deliberately destroyed in 1933; the same was done with the cattle in the drought of 1934; later on, thousands of tons of potatoes and oranges and millions of eggs were ruined for human consumption. The inflation, both of labor costs and living costs, which we thus legislated was supposed to be temporary; it soon became a permanent national policy.

Only the onset of the second World War rescued the New Deal from its economic *auto da fé*, providing jobs for additional millions of workers in uniform or in munitions plants and shipyards, and setting up an inexhaustible demand for the production of expensive industrial products which could be shot away or blown up or sunk in the sea with no corresponding economic benefit to our society.

A scarcity of labor was created by the manpower demands of a war which kept fifteen million Americans in the armed forces and swiftly liquidated the construction which the New Deal had started with the Civilian Con-

servation Corps, public works, and the work-relief program. It was much more exciting to fight the Nazis than
to plant trees, terrace hillsides, or build houses.

Even the most brilliant and controversial of the New
Deal projects—the Tennessee Valley Authority and the
great dams on the Columbia River—no longer were
valued primarily for their social and economic benefit to
the people of the regions they served. They were valued
chiefly as sources of industrial power for our war plants,
especially for the development of the atom bomb at Oak
Ridge, Tennessee and Hanford, Washington. For the
most audacious of all Roosevelt's successful programs,
the development of atomic energy, blossomed only in a
frightful weapon of indiscriminate slaughter. Had he
succeeded in persuading Congress to authorize the St.
Lawrence Seaway and the Florida Ship Canal or tidal
power at Passamaquoddy, these in turn would have
found their justification in helping us stoke the fantastic
destruction of global warfare.

As a result of the growing danger of World War III,
today destruction threatens even the vestiges of these
imaginative programs—for the benefit of union labor,
commercial farming, a restricted variety of social security, and hydroelectric development. The good fruit
of the New Deal's domestic program is today corrupted
by the evil fruit of the New Deal's foreign policy.

What use to have your pay docked, year after year, for
compulsory old-age savings and unemployment insur-

ance when inflation steals half the value of your pension and when you may not live to enjoy it?

Of what avail will be social security and old-age pensions, farm-benefit payments and price supports, collective bargaining and higher wages, if the American people—old and young, farmer and factory hand—are exposed to sudden death from the skies?

What good will be the great dams of the Far West except to provide conspicuous targets for atomic bombers? What use is a good industrial pension plan if your factory is blown up? Of what value a guaranteed price for wheat, if your sons are in the army? What price your social security card against a Communist tank in Korea or on the Elbe?

What good will it do a man to refinance his mortgage or live in a low-rent public housing project if the cities must be evacuated in the name of civil defense?

For the Roosevelt administration followed a foreign policy which has placed all of its domestic reforms in jeopardy. Today, as the Republicans take over the established programs for social welfare and economic justice which an entire generation of Americans labored to create, the growing threat of a third world war hints that, like the rubble of Berlin and Hiroshima, they too may be laid waste.

Twenty years ago, Roosevelt offered to the American people the promise of a more abundant life. Today, the children of the Forgotten Man of 1933 live under the shadow of the more abundant death.

2. THE "INCREDIBLE" DURKIN

The most ironic captive of the Democratic munitions economy is that minority of our working people which calls itself "labor." Of the sixty million Americans who work for a living, about fifteen million, or one quarter, are members of labor unions. Their votes kept the Democrats in office for years and the war and post-war defense crisis conferred upon them phenomenal power.

In time of national emergency, the right to strike became the power to sabotage national security; elaborate governmental and legal precautions have been needed to hold this dangerous power within bounds. It was obviously flattering to union leaders to have their mundane demands for more money for less work exalted to the level of world politics and the survival of human freedom. They groaned but they loved it. Yet, if peace should break out, their power and prestige would be swiftly deflated. Strikes would be settled on their economic merits rather than on the basis of public safety. There would also be heavy unemployment. Between a quarter and a third of current economic activity is now related to defense. With peace and the demobilization of the three and a half million Americans now in our armed forces, a cutback in defense spending could produce a major crisis in employment.

An example of this process of union deflation is already visible in the case of the Transport Workers Union in New York City. By their votes they have controlled the city government which owns the subways. By their wage demands they have forced the city transportation system to lose money. Finally, they came to the point of demanding that either the city tax all the other working people in order to raise the wages of a small group of workers or that the fare be raised, costing the average city family well over fifty dollars extra each year.

This self-defeating conclusion to the cycle of wage demands and voting strength is also duplicated in the national defense program, where the Federal Government taxes all the working people to underwrite high wage scales for the minority of workers employed in the coal, steel, automotive, chemical, electric, and related munitions industries. If this forced market should be blitzed by peace, defense contracts would be cut back or cancelled, and with them the means to pay high wages and maintain full employment at the expense of the taxpayers would dwindle.

This, rather than the barren bickering over repeal or modification of the Taft-Hartley Labor-Management Law, is the basic issue which confronts Eisenhower's Secretary of Labor, the "incredible" Martin P. Durkin of Chicago. Mr. Durkin is a quiet, ascetic plumber, who neither smokes, drinks, nor swears, and one of whose three sons is preparing to enter the Catholic priesthood. Durkin is a Democrat who supported Stevenson and is an opponent of the Taft-Hartley Law; when "Ike" announced the appointment, Senator Taft exclaimed, "Incredible!" It was politically believable when you examined the facts of the case.

Durkin owes his job to the fact that he is *not* a Protestant. As "Ike" was completing his cabinet it was suddenly realized that he didn't have a single Catholic in any major administration job. Something had to be done, fast. Herbert Brownell got in touch with the National Catholic Welfare Conference at Washington, and came back with the name of Durkin. So that was that.

Secretary Durkin is nearly sixty and started his working career as a steamfitter's apprentice in Chicago in 1911. He served with the field artillery and the cavalry in France during the first World War, and when he returned from overseas he became Chicago business manager of the Plumbers Union—or as they prefer to be called, the United Association of Journeymen and Apprentices in the Plumbing and Pipe-fitting Industry of United States and Canada, A. F. of L. He held that job for twenty years, with no nonsense about union democracy, until he was promoted to be secretary-treasurer of the whole international union in 1941, and moved to Washington. Two years later he became the plumbers' president, a post which he held until he entered the cabinet, and conducted their business so efficiently that he drew an anti-trust prosecution from the government. Of course, the charge was not pressed, but it was a sort of economic accolade.

Shortly after taking residence in wartime Washington, Durkin became associated with the National Catholic Welfare Conference and was made vice-president of the Catholic Conference on Industrial Problems. This means that he is an adherent of the Vatican-sponsored program for a corporative organization of industry along the lines pioneered by Dr. Salazar in Portugal—a notably non-industrial but completely Catholic country—and a devotee of the papal encyclicals on social justice. This ecclesiastical program involves the self-regulation of industry by labor-management councils; it is opposed to state socialism and labor syndicalism, as well as to Communism; it involves such concepts as the family wage and the annual wage and so offers a middle way between conventional Anglo-Saxon trade-unionism and the Communist-Nazi type of labor-front organization.

When Durkin was appointed, the current Washington jibe ran that "Ike's" Cabinet consisted of eight millionaires and one plumber. Apart from the fact that at least two of the other cabinet officers could not qualify as millionaires, the gloss on this quip pointed out that the plumbers were the wealthiest group of American property owners, because by the time a plumber had done a job on you, he not only owned his own home, but owned your house as well.

Durkin's approach to the job was characteristically conciliatory. He began by reassuring the staff of the Labor Department that they need not fear dismissal because of having been originally appointed by Democrats. He fell flat on his face when he tried to take up the Taft-Hartley law, and his political future is cloudy. But in his dealings with Senator Taft he showed good humor and courtesy, and it could fairly be said that his appointment by "Ike" was justified if only because it reassured the jittery union leaders that they would not be subject to reprisals by the incoming Republicans.

3. SINCLAIR WEEKS

As individuals, the businessmen of the country remembered how they had been pushed around for twenty years, derided and chided at the same time they were told to go out and earn more profits to be taxed for support of a government which they were accused of having mismanaged.

After being the target of such political propaganda for a generation and being forced by such statutes as section 7A of the National Industrial Recovery Act of 1933 and the Wagner Act of 1935 to grant what they regarded as unjustified and unwise power to labor unions, they had become almost pathological in their dislike for government regulations and organized labor. They clung bitterly to the small relief they had been granted by the Taft-Hartley Law of 1947, and they nursed a sense of grievance against the big labor leaders, especially John L. Lewis of the United Mine Workers and President Philip Murray of the Congress of Industrial Organizations. The deaths of both Murray and President William Green of the A. F. of L. shortly after "Ike's" election seemed to symbolize the idea that it was "time for a change," and they were eager to make the change swiftly.

In addition, they—far more than labor—were uneasily aware that their profits and production depended largely on government defense spending. They realized, as labor did not, that in 1940, after eight years of the New Deal, there had still been ten million Americans unemployed, and that it was only the war which provided full employment at high wages. They, too, were the prisoners of the Fair Deal barracks society, and knew that cessation of foreign aid or a cutback in defense appropriations could send many prosperous concerns to the wall. They did not propose to be trapped by rigid wages and controlled prices in the recession which all business economists warned might follow a basic change in defense policy. Yet here again the mood of many businessmen was complicated by their traditional isolationism and their dislike of a foreign policy which had involved their fortunes so deeply in world events. This whole set of psychological factors in the business community called for the services of a first-rate family doctor with a good bedside manner and a little black bag.

That need was fittingly supplied by Eisenhower's choice of Sinclair Weeks of Massachusetts as his Secretary of Commerce. This appointment was a big political surprise. Before "Ike's" nomination, Weeks had been strongly supported by the Dewey Republicans for the post of national chairman. In the maneuvering at the Chicago convention it became necessary to sidetrack his candidacy in order to win the support of Michigan's Republican state chairman, Arthur Summerfield. However, when "Ike" gave Summerfield the traditional party management job of Postmaster-General, Weeks was offered his choice between the Commerce Department and the vacated position of Republican national chairman. Most insiders assumed he would take the chairmanship. Instead, he plumped for the cabinet and thus cleared the way for Wes Roberts at the national committee.

Weeks is a member of an old-established conservative Boston banking family. His father served as Secretary of War in Harding's cabinet and the family firm of Hornblower & Weeks was one of the financial giants of the 1920's. Sinclair Weeks himself was born in West Newton, Massachusetts, sixty years ago, graduated from Harvard in 1914, and married a year later. He is the father of six children and, like most proper Bostonians, a thoroughly dependable family man. During the first World War, he served with the field artillery, fighting in France all through 1918, from the German March offensive to the armistice.

Except for that martial interlude, he remained with the family financial business for ten years until he branched out into manufacturing in 1923. In addition to a connection with the Reed & Barton silver business at Taunton, Massachusetts, he has been especially active in the United Carr Fastener Corporation of Cambridge, Massachusetts, an eminently successful "holding company" which makes every kind of fastener except zippers.

About the same time that he went into manufacturing, Weeks also entered politics, starting as alderman of Newton and later serving as its mayor for three terms. In 1944, Leverett Saltonstall, who was then the Bay State's governor, appointed him to serve in the Senate for a few months after Cabot Lodge resigned. For many years, Weeks was also active on the Massachusetts Republican state committee and on the Republican national committee. He was G.O.P. committeeman from Massachusetts for twelve years, served as the national committee's treasurer for three years, and was chairman of the party's finance committee from 1949 until he entered "Ike's" Cabinet.

Weeks was a tower of strength in the Eisenhower movement before and at Chicago, and went on to give "Ike" full financial and political support in the 1952 campaign. He is one of the tough breed of Yankee busi-

nessmen who have shown that they can survive Democrats and depressions without whining. One of his first
statements after entering the cabinet was to suggest that,
after so many years of special Federal devotion to cotton
and rayon, maybe it was time to do something for wool.
New England's famous old woolen industry has, in fact,
been neglected for forty years and the old sheep farms
have been abandoned, but the woolen mills and the skill
are still there. Why not revive it?

In spite of southern shudders at the thought, Weeks'
proposal contains a good deal of economic sense. At the
very least, it is an indication of his New England tenacity
and his political acumen that he should counter the
southward drift of the cotton mills from New England
by a return to Yankee first principles.

The Department of Commerce, which he now heads,
has of course fallen from its high estate under Herbert
Hoover. After being administered by Dan Roper and
Charles Sawyer, there wasn't much left of the original
Republican dream of a "normalcy" in which American
businessmen, by seeking to enrich themselves, would remake the world. But American businessmen are again
coming back into repute and power and Sinclair Weeks
is one of the best of them: a man who understands both
business and politics and can make the two of them trot
together in double harness even as in the sunny decades
before the first World War.

4. "Cousin Ezra"

Before anything like that can happen, something must be done about the farmers. When Roosevelt took the dollar off the gold standard, he tried to put our money on a commodity basis through his so-called "parity price formula." Under this policy, a bushel of wheat or corn, or a bale of cotton, was supposed to have a constant purchasing power in terms of the cost of the manufactured goods the farmers must buy.

The initial attempt to bring this to pass meant, in fact, a sharp reduction in the supply of farm products. Acreage allotments and marketing quotas; commodity-loan programs; Agricultural Conservation Program payments; slaughter of pigs and cattle; and the diversion of excess food into domestic relief and foreign channels under the commodity purchase programs—all was part of a costly combination resulting at times in depriving the American people and the world of the benefits of our own agricultural abundance in attempting to increase farm income by creating an artificial scarcity.

With the war, high inflexible price supports, ninety per cent. of parity, were relied upon to stimulate the very production which had previously been curtailed. With half the world to feed, this made sense. When the war ended, however, the price supports, high and inflexible, were continued long after they were needed, since the wartime demand for agricultural commodities had subsided. As the years passed, the rest of the world resumed its production of food and our foreign markets contracted, except as we were willing to give away our produce. There was a slow decline in farm prices because of artificially stimulated high production due to the guarantee of high price supports, and the government was compelled to buy up more and more, not only crops such as cotton and grain, which could be safely stored, but products which deteriorated rapidly, such as potatoes and butter. By the time Eisenhower took over, the Department of Agriculture, operating under a system of high inflexible price supports, had invested over a billion dollars of public money to hold up the price of vital food and related products to our people, buying and storing on a compulsory basis the following sizable inventory:

> 70 million pounds of butter
> 265 million bushels of corn
> 125 million bushels of wheat
> 97 million pounds of peanuts
> 23 million pounds of cheddar cheese
> 525 million gallons of turpentine
> 96 million pounds of dried milk
> 2 million bales of cotton
> 186 million pounds of linseed oil
> 165 million pounds of rosin
> 421 million pounds of cottonseed oil
> 130,000 pounds of wool

4 million pounds of tobacco
150 million pounds of beans

In addition to all this, the department in a single year spent additional millions of dollars to hold up the price of eggs, pork, pears, apples, cherries, orange juice, turkeys, almonds, prunes, raisins, and honey.

Here was the guarantee of legislated price inflation. As industrial prices rose, due to defense contracts and Federal taxes, the price-support program required higher farm prices. Higher food prices meant demands for higher wages. Higher wages meant higher industrial costs and prices, and so on. More important still was the fact that farmers hold the political balance of power in the Senate and in most of the states and, despite a sharp decline in the number of farm families, could block any legislative change in this system.

Yet if peace should come and we should curtail our system of foreign subsidies, the export market would decline still further, domestic purchasing power would be reduced, and still larger and less manageable food surpluses would accumulate.

To deal with this splitting economic headache, "Ike" turned to the Church of Jesus Christ of Latter-Day Saints, commonly known as the Mormon Church, and appointed one of its twelve apostles, fifty-four-year-old Ezra Taft Benson of Idaho, as his Secretary of Agriculture. This selection paid long overdue tribute to the agricultural genius of the Latter-Day Saints, who after thriving in Illinois and Iowa, were driven west into the Utah Desert by savage persecution. By a combination of cooperation, church discipline, and the inspired leadership of Brigham Young, the Mormons over the years literally have made the desert blossom like the rose. Their probity, ability, and self-reliance have contributed increasingly to the whole nation.

Benson, by his own admission to "Ike," had been a preconvention Taft supporter, although he had previously supported Dewey in '44 and '48. When the Taftites sought to console themselves for the large Dewey influence in "Ike's" Cabinet, they joked, "Well, we still have Cousin Ezra!" Ezra Taft Benson, however, is no close relation to the Ohio Senator, being a sixth cousin. He was born in the little Idaho town of Whitney, a great-grandson of the original Mormon Apostle, Ezra Taft Benson, who pioneered with Brigham Young and entered the Salt Lake Valley with that remarkable man in 1847. The new secretary's parents were pioneer settlers in southern Idaho, where he grew up on a farm and ran it for several years. He graduated from the Utah State Agricultural College in 1921 and, like many young Mormons, spent two years in church missionary service in the British Isles.

Ezra Benson continued his studies on his return, graduating with honors from Brigham Young University at Provo, Utah, taking a master's degree in agricultural economics at Iowa State University, and doing graduate work at the University of California as late as 1938. In between times he served as an extension-service county agent in Idaho and as a specialist on farm marketing at the University of Idaho, where he became head of the department of agricultural economics and marketing. This position led him into the farm co-operative movement, so congenial to the Mormon tradition of co-operation, and he achieved national distinction in this field, rising to be chairman of the American Institute of Co-operation, which includes some fifteen hundred co-operative and related farm organizations. Benson also is active in the Mormon Church, having become in 1943 a member of the Council of the (12) Apostles, the governing body of that church. After the second World War, the church sent him to Europe in charge of its European mission; he spent nearly a year traveling some sixty thousand miles on Mormon relief work in the war-torn countries.

There is no doubt that Ezra Benson has accepted his cabinet post with a sense of religious dedication. He feels that his appointment is a distinct tribute to his church and his friends feel that he, as a Mormon, has much to offer the American farmers of all faiths. Mormons believe in work—the beehive is the symbol of their home state, Utah—and in co-operation and mutual help rather than in charity, subsidy, or handouts. If Secretary Benson can lift our agriculture out of the bureaucratic and financial swamp created by his predecessors of late years and the philosophy under which they have operated, with their seventy thousand officials and their collectivist plans to pay the farmer to take orders from Washington and vote for the party in power, it is a sure bet that he will need the help of Almighty God. It is part of Benson's strength that he believes he will receive divine assistance.

5. OVETA CULP HOBBY

That something must be done to break the rising spiral of food prices has long been recognized by sociologists and welfare workers. The entire Federal social security system, which collects over three billion dollars a year in payroll taxes to finance old-age pensions and unemployment pay, has been subverted by the inflated cost of living. To put it plainly, in the 1930's people were taxed in dollars which were worth considerably more than the dollars they get back in the 1950's, and so cannot provide for their needs. The social security system itself became a useful Democratic device to enforce the payroll withholding tax, while the social security fund, which was to have been a trust for the benefit of the aged and the unemployed, has in practice become just a small part of the general receipts of the United States Treasury. After it had experienced the services of two eminent Democratic politicians, Paul McNutt of Indiana and Oscar Ewing of New York, "Ike" thought it was time for a good housecleaning in the Federal Security Administration and appointed a woman as its chief, Colonel Oveta Culp Hobby of Houston, Texas. From the start, Colonel Hobby had a seat at cabinet meetings and her agency was promptly made a full Department of Health, Education, and Welfare, with general responsibility for the government's program for education and social welfare.

Although the colonel is nationally famous as wartime commander of the Woman's Army Corps, in Texas she is famous as a newspaper editor and publisher and as a politician. Oveta Culp was born at Killeen, Texas, 48 years ago, and first made her mark as parliamentarian of the Texas House of Legislature in 1926–31. At the end of that period she made an unanswerable point of order by marrying the former Governor of Texas, William Pettis Hobby. She has two children and is herself a strikingly handsome brunette with a first-class brain. Her brain was soon put to work on her husband's paper, the Houston *Post*, where she gradually rose from the job of research editor in 1931 to that of editor and publisher in 1952.

During the war, Mrs. Hobby came to Washington, first with Army Public Relations, and then as commandant of the Women's Auxiliary Army Corps, later the WACs, with the rank of colonel. At the end of this service, she was duly given the Distinguished Service Medal, and returned to her editorial desk at Houston. She learned all one needs to know about the Washington runaround in her days at the Pentagon.

Her presence in the cabinet is due, not only to her beauty, influence, or experience as an administrator; it is also a Republican debt of political gratitude to the Lone Star State for having voted for "Ike." Texas still retains the old frontier attitude toward initiative and self-reliance, and Colonel Hobby's career reflects that Texas tradition. She is smart, she is tactful, and she knows her stuff.

If full-scale war or peace should complicate the social problems of the millions of Americans under the eye of her department, one can be sure that she will handle them chiefly by calling on private initiative and local agencies to co-operate, rather than slap down a dramatic new program, demand a big new Congressional appropriation, and hire thousands of additional government employees to put it across. The model of social welfare established by Governor Dewey in New York and reinforced by Eisenhower's determination to put it on a pay-as-you-go basis, rather than Oscar Ewing's sweeping proposals for nationalized medicine and Federal control of education, will be her preference. Hers is the chance to show what the Republicans meant when they said "We can do it better!" New York, for example, has a far more advanced program for health, welfare, and security than any state in the Union, and far in advance of anything yet done in Washington. Other Republican states have made similar progress and have done so without bureaucracy or regimentation, also with great economy and flexibility. This is where the Eisenhower administration can make real social history in the nation; it looks as though they intended to do so.

6. THE MOST REPRESENTATIVE MAN

The Interior Department is another branch of the Federal Government where the New Republicans intend to show that they can do it better. Here the chief issue centers around land use and public power projects, mainly in the Far West; big, costly multi-purpose dams which will help meet the expected ten years of continued power shortage in the enormous region between the Rocky Mountains and the Pacific.

"Ike" has put just about the most representative Republican in his administration in charge of this controversial program, a westerner whose first decision was to disappoint the small but vocal group which hailed "Ike's" victory as a mandate to stop all the talk about putting the Federal Government into the power business.

The former Governor of Oregon, Douglas McKay, may have received his job in recognition for the man-sized job done for "Ike" by Oregon state chairman Ralph Cake in the 1952 campaign, but he is entitled to recognition in his own right. So typical is McKay of the kind of New Republican Eisenhower has brought to Washington—or who brought Eisenhower to Washington—that it is worth taking an extended look at his career.

He was born in Portland, Oregon, in 1893, the son of a carpenter of Scottish descent with a touch of Dutch blood, and of a Scottish mother with a dash of French ancestry. All of his four grandparents arrived in Oregon by 1852, seven years before the territory became a state. By heritage, he is part of the old West of the Oregon Trail and the covered wagons.

As soon as he was thirteen, young McKay started working after school to help support the family; each summer he worked on a farm near the little Oregon country town of Scappoose. He had a strong liking for farming and at the age of eighteen dropped out of high school in order to enter the agricultural course at the Oregon State College at Corvallis, where he first showed his knack at politics by getting himself elected as president of the freshman class.

He worked his way through college, paying his own tuition and contributing to family income as well, and graduated in 1917, qualified as a county agricultural agent. He never got the job. By then we had entered World War I and he left Corvallis to go to officer's training school at the Presidio in San Francisco shortly after his marriage to Miss Mabel C. Hill, a stenographer whom he had met in a Portland law office. After some basic training he was sent to France as a second lieutenant with the 361st Infantry and, during the battle for Sedan in the Meuse-Argonne offensive, suffered a serious shell wound which changed his whole career.

Hit in six places in the right shoulder, McKay almost lost his arm, but a series of operations enabled him to regain use of his shoulder muscles, and he was discharged as cured. However, the injury forced him to give up farming, for which he had trained, and to seek a less arduous occupation. After a try at selling insurance and automobiles, he became sales manager of a Portland motor company and was assigned to his firm's Chevrolet agency in Salem, the state capital.

That was in 1927, the first year that Chevrolet outdistanced Ford, and he soon set up in business for himself, forming the Douglas McKay Chevrolet Company. His business prospered and eventually, in 1946, he was able to move into a large new building of his own and handle both Chevrolets and Cadillacs. For this success as a salesman he has been charged with being a puppet of General Motors!

He is nobody's puppet. His political career shows that he can succeed independently without regard to Detroit. For example, in 1932 he was elected mayor of Salem and kept the city on a hand-to-mouth basis during the two worst years of the depression. Because his own business barely kept out of the red during this same period, McKay came to a sound Scottish conclusion: that it is the duty of government, as well as business, to preserve and guard its financial foundation. So he went into state politics and was elected state senator in 1934, being re-elected four times in succession, each time leading the rest of the Republican county ticket.

As a state legislator, McKay specialized on highway planning, as was natural in an automobile dealer, particularly after World War II, a period when all states faced crucial decisions involving the rebuilding and rehabilitation of all public works, including their highway systems. He took his political life in his hands at this time, risked bitter conflict with powerful selfish interests, and floated bonds and rebuilt the roads. He also was interested in conservation, backed the Willamette Valley project and championed the Willamette River Basin Commission. He entered national politics in 1940 when he campaigned for Wendell Willkie. He helped Dewey win the Republican Presidential nomination in 1948, and in 1952 played a useful part of lining up West Coast delegates for Eisenhower at Chicago.

Where was he in 1944? On the day the Japanese attacked Pearl Harbor, December 7th, 1941, McKay happened to be in Honolulu with the Willamette University football team, and he and the squad helped dig trenches on that "day of infamy." He immediately volunteered for active military service but his World War I wound confined him to limited duty. He was commissioned captain in October of 1942, being later promoted to major, and served as public-relations officer at Camp Murray and Camp Adair.

At the end of the war he went back to Oregon politics

and was elected the forty-ninth governor of Oregon in the 1948 election.

Of course he's a joiner; that is part of the western tradition in business and politics. By the latest count, he belongs to the Veterans of Foreign Wars, the Disabled American Veterans, the American Legion, the Masons, the Shriners, the Knight Templars, Kiwanis, Elks, and Eagles. He is also an active and devout Presbyterian. He and his wife have two daughters; a son was killed in an automobile accident while a student at Oregon State University. One of his daughters, incidentally, is taking up her father's lost career in agriculture and is studying to become a farm expert. His favorite hobby, which is also in the western tradition, is horseback riding.

In short, Douglas McKay is just about the most average kind of small-town business man in politics who ever came down the Potomac. Slender, dark and alert at sixty, he could serve as a stand-in for almost any cabinet officer in "Ike's" administration and would do a pretty competent job. He rounds out the Eisenhower group which has accepted the receivership of the windy, contradictory, costly, and controversial legacy of Democratic social and economic reform.

It speaks much for Roosevelt's political skill, although not for his national statesmanship, that he gave the country the impression that he and the Democratic Party had invented and patented all the social progress in the United States. Actually, the New Deal derived most of its social-welfare program from New York State, where a long series of progressive governors, Republican and Democratic (including Teddy Roosevelt, Charles Evans Hughes, Charles Whitman, and the great Al Smith), had been dealing for decades with the emerging problem of an industrial and urban society in a country which was originally composed of farmers and traders. The vice of the Roosevelt trick was that it persuaded many Republicans that their party must oppose necessary measures of adjustment and reform and even led them to attack members of their own party who dared to continue the Republican tradition of social progress and economic fair play.

The Eisenhower group *can* do it better if they simply pick up where Roosevelt left off and go to New York and other progressive commonwealths to study and adapt the steady, undramatic, sensible measures which such Republican governors as Dewey, Duff, Driscoll, and McKay have enacted and administered. The truth is that there is no single broad national solution for any of our social problems. Living conditions, climate, custom, population, and economic circumstances vary tremendously from state to state and from region to region. The Republican solution is to find ways to adjust flexible national programs to local and regional differences. This method distrusts hordes of officials and doubts the efficacy of enormous Federal appropriations, preferring to rely on private and local agencies and to confine Federal action to helping local authorities to solve their local problems. That is where the New Deal reforms went astray and that is where the New Republicans can bring the country up to date with its own remarkable progress if they are not interrupted by war.

Their greatest weakness is that, with certain exceptions, the New Republicans seem to lack human kindness. Where such Democrats as "Al" Smith in New York and "Ed" Kelly in Chicago were deeply concerned with the problems and frailties of their constituents, the Republicans often fail to consider the happiness or sorrows of their neighbors. This lack is what St. Paul meant when he said that if you have not charity, all else faileth, and is responsible for the charges of arrogance and indifference to human needs which have accompanied past Republican defeats. The New Republicans have succeeded and are legitimately proud of their success, but it is only as they have individually suffered or failed that they show an understanding of the fact that, in American politics, it is not enough to serve your fellow-men: you must also like them.

VIII

NEW BROOMS

1. ORPHAN OF THE ADMINISTRATION

NOT the least of the ironies of the Eisenhower administration is the part played by the Department of Justice.

During the 1952 campaign, "the mess in Washington" seemed to guarantee that the Attorney General of the United States would occupy the best political showcase in the country. The nation had been startled by a rash of resounding scandals, involving graft and corruption throughout the Truman administration: five-percenters, mink coats, R.F.C. favoritism in granting loans, blackmail and thieving in the Bureau of Internal Revenue, stealing in the Commodity Credit Corporation, and a blind eye to all these doings on the part of the Department of Justice. "Turn the rascals out!" is always effective politics and a large amount of the moral fervor mobilized in support of "Ike's" crusade stemmed from public disgust with the Democratic clique which had grown old, fat, contented, and corrupt in national office.

Eisenhower's decision to appoint the man whom Governor Dewey regarded as one of the most brilliant political brains in the United States, Mr. Herbert Brownell, as his Attorney General implied that the Department of Justice would set the pace for the whole new administration. A record for vigorous, intelligent, and successful housecleaning and prosecution at Washington could place Brownell before the country in the finest possible light. His ability and honesty were acknowledged and widely respected by lawyers and politicians alike. He had been Dewey's partner in politics for a quarter of a century and held the unequaled record of having successfully managed the nomination of three successive Republican Presidential candidates. He was "Ike's" key man in clearing applicants for policymaking jobs in the incoming Republican administration. He had selected young, able, decent men as his assistants and was expected to make political, as well as legal, history on the Potomac.

Unfortunately for these great and justified expectations, "the mess in Washington" proved to be a great deal more serious than any number of mink coats on the wrong backs or wads of money in the wrong pockets. Top billing in the new Republican show reflected the basic problems before the country: foreign policy, defense and taxation. The limelight was focused on John Foster Dulles, Charles E. Wilson, George M. Humphrey, and their assistants in the departments of State, Defense, and Treasury, for the duration of the world crisis with which the Eisenhower administration found itself desperately engaged.

In fact, instead of dealing with the problem of corruption in government, the new Attorney General's first assignment was to devise acceptable methods for handling the unfamiliar problems involved in dealing with matters of security, loyalty, and subversion.

During the long Hoover depression a good many generous, idealistic young Americans became disillusioned by the scandalous breakdown of our economic system and were attracted by the communistic urge of the Marxist doctrine. They were also favorably impressed by Russia's tremendous drive and direction under Stalinist state-planning and saw no harm in embracing theoretical Communism as a tenable political faith. Added to them, of course, was the sizable group of low-caliber citizens who in any country and in any age will always sell their mother's back teeth for the price of a drink; the two sets became the basis for an extremely efficient Soviet spy service in the United States. Before and during the war, that situation did not seem to matter. We had recognized Russia in 1933, as part of Roosevelt's diplomatic reaction to the rise of Hitler, and in our conduct of the war the Red army necessarily became a vital element in our military strategy and planning. It was only after V-J Day that we became uneasily aware of the fact that the Kremlin had planted its agents and sympathizers throughout the Federal Government. The country had belatedly taken panicky alarm and was in a mood to approve far-reaching investigations of public officials, public entertainers, schoolteachers, scientists, and professors. Yet there was no clear precedent for appropriate action in this legal no-man's land. The entire problem was foreign to the spirit of our laws and institutions.

Granted that it is the responsibility of the Chief Executive to ascertain the loyalty and reliability of government employees, could an official charged with being a poor security risk have resort to the courts or invoke the principles of the Bill of Rights? If so, what became of our basic governmental principle of the "division of powers"? If not, what guarantee was there that a man unjustly accused could establish his innocence? Two convicted Soviet spies involved in the theft of American atomic secrets for the benefit of the Kremlin faced death by electrocution. Their action was punishable by death under the Espionage Act of 1917. Should the Department of Justice recommend clemency and thus cater to the world-wide organized Communist agitation for the pardon of the two spies? Or should the Attorney General advise the President to let the law take its course and countenance the creation of two more Communist "martyrs"?

Granted that the Department of Justice could devise some satisfactory plan for dealing with the loyalty of Federal employees, what protection could it offer to applicants for Federal employment? If an individual official was entitled to a hearing on charges of disloyalty, could a man or woman unjustly accused of disloyalty be black-listed for appointment without an equal opportunity to establish the falsity of malicious accusations?

Such issues, rather than the classic performance of a new broom making a clean sweep of dust and cobwebs, became part of the administrative maze in which the new Attorney General and his assistants found themselves the moment they had taken their oaths of office. For these were parts of the police problem imposed on the nation by its foreign situation and, although they had no coun-terpart in the normal traditions of American jurispru-dence, were closely related to the brute question of American survival in the face of the clear and present danger from abroad.

2. HERBERT BROWNELL, JR.

Ever since the 1952 elections, the Democrats have said that Governor Dewey of New York is the ablest politi-cal leader in the United States. Dewey would deny the accuracy of this tribute to his skill and judgment in pub-lic affairs on the ground that Brownell has the better claim. Of course, the fact of the matter is that Dewey is the administrator of public office and Brownell the po-litical manager. As a matter of record, the two men have worked together as a team so long that it is almost im-possible to say where one begins and the other leaves off in their combined operations.

Certainly, any list of "Ike's" kingmakers could not omit Brownell, who handled the grinding detail work of Eisenhower's pre-convention campaign and managed the in-fighting at the nominating convention itself. And when "Ike" picked Brownell as his Attorney General, most people assumed that it was a political reward for these services.

They overlooked the fact that Brownell is an able lawyer in his own right and that his political activities have almost literally been conducted in his spare time. Like "Ike," he is a prairie product. His father was a professor at the University of Nebraska and the future Attorney General was born in the little town of Peru, Nebraska, attended the public schools, and graduated from the state university with a Phi Beta Kappa key in 1924. Like Dewey, he then came east to study law and received his law degree, with honors, from Yale in 1927. That same year he passed the New York bar examinations and joined the conservative Wall Street law firm of Root, Clark, Buckner, Howland, and Ballentine. The year of the panic he changed to the long-established firm of Lord, Day, and Lord, remaining with them until he came to Washington with "Ike" twenty-four years later. His specialty is hotel law and he is expert in keeping his clients out of court and protecting their good name without unnecessary litigation.

The same year that he became a partner of Lord, Day, and Lord he married Miss Doris McCarter of Texas. The

Brownells have four children, are Methodists and in every way conform to the New Republican model of family life and undramatic, solid achievement.

Brownell's political career began in 1931, as did that of so many younger Republicans. The depression had shaken the complacency out of the G.O.P. and the same ferment which created the New Deal was also distilling its political antidote. Brownell was Republican district captain in New York's old 10th Manhattan Assembly District, a closely divided district then held by Tammany Hall. Another captain in the same district was named Tom Dewey and when Brownell decided to run for the assembly in 1931, Dewey was his campaign manager. That year he lost to a Roosevelt Democrat, Langdon Post, but in 1932 Brownell ran again and was elected, because Tammany decided to knife Post for having supported the Seabury investigation. However, the political climate of New York City was changing. In 1933, Fiorello LaGuardia, a progressive Republican, was elected Mayor and Brownell remained in the state assembly for five consecutive terms.

This record effectively disposes of the quip that Brownell's political experience has been confined to rounding up delegates to Republican national conventions who do not wish to vote for Robert A. Taft. By 1942, Dewey and Brownell had reversed their roles and it was Herb Brownell who acted as Dewey's campaign manager when Dewey was elected as the first Republican governor of the Empire State in twenty years. His brilliance is attested to by the impressive fact that his candidates won the Republican Presidential nomination against powerful opposition in 1944, 1948, and 1952. After Dewey's foredoomed defeat by Roosevelt in 1944, Brownell served as Republican national chairman for a couple of years. After Dewey's unexpected defeat by Truman in the "surprise election" of 1948, many Republicans blamed Brownell for the policy of "dignity and unity" which bred a disastrous political complacency. Brownell particularly irritated many Midwest Republicans and his name, like Dewey's, was a red flag to the Taft supporters in 1952. An expert behind-the-scenes political operator, Brownell ran rings around some of the more mentally muscle-bound opponents of General Eisenhower. His role before and at the convention was that of chief of staff and his strategy paid off in "Ike's" first-ballot nomination.

During the contest with Adlai Stevenson, Brownell worked inconspicuously at "Ike's" Hotel Commodore headquarters in New York. This was the period when Eisenhower soft-pedaled his Dewey connections in order to cultivate the good will of the bruised and embittered Taftites. Brownell showed that he could learn by experience and, whereas in 1948 the Republicans had been destroyed by overconfidence, he used the clamor over the Taft-Ike axis to induce a corresponding mood of "It's in the bag" among the doomed Democrats. The payoff came on election day when "Ike" received the greatest popular majority of any Republican President and New York State itself gave him an unprecedented plurality of over eight hundred and forty thousand votes.

Brownell's political future, like Dewey's, is a legitimate subject for speculation. If a peaceful accommodation of interests should end the "cold-war" crisis, his task of clean-up man in the Augean stables of Fair Deal politics in the Justice Department would confer upon him the same kind of national prominence achieved by Dewey as "racket-buster" in New York City twenty years ago.

However, if the East-West conflict persists, Brownell's role may easily parallel that of his Democratic predecessors, such as Robert Jackson or Francis Biddle.

In any case, it is far and high for a boy from the Nebraska prairies to have traveled before his fiftieth year. His career is concrete evidence that ours is still a society of opportunity and that the practice of law is still the key which opens most of the doors to success in public life.

3. The F.B.I.—Tail or Dog?

On Brownell and his assistants depends the not unimportant question of whether we shall develop along police-state lines, whether the F.B.I. shall wag the dog in a government supposedly of laws, not men.

Will the symbol of American justice be the blindfolded goddess with the scales and sword, or will it be the omnipotent G-man, with his files, his fingerprints and his shoulder holster?

So far as "Ike's" Attorney General is concerned, the answer is clear. It is provided by the group of lawyers he has brought in to help him make a clean sweep of the fixes and other ward-politics practices which crept into the Department of Justice after Truman made Tom Clark of Texas his Attorney General. Brownell's Deputy Attorney General is forty-year-old William P. Rogers, born in the little town of Norfolk, New York, and a graduate of Colgate who received his law degree from Cornell. Bill Rogers got his start in New York City as assistant District Attorney in 1938 under Tom Dewey. A member of a big Wall Street law firm, he also served as chief counsel for the Senate War Investigating Committee at Washington after a good war record in the navy. During the 1952 campaign, Rogers rode the Nixon train and is credited with extricating the Republican Vice-Presidential candidate from the famous "Nixon Fund" Democratic smear. Rogers is no innocent in politics and promptly appointed a Taft Republican as his assistant, thirty-four-year-old Robert Minor of Columbus, Ohio, who had been Senator John Bricker's administrative assistant.

The same pattern of political prudence and careful selection of qualified young lawyers was followed in the other Department of Justice key jobs. They all follow the New Republican pattern: all family men, all young for politics.

There remains the shadowy "Fourth Branch of American Government," the Federal Bureau of Investigation. Under the long, honest, and efficient direction of J. Edgar Hoover, the F.B.I. has achieved much of the prestige with Congress and the public enjoyed by the Marine Corps. It has kept out of politics and has avoided scandal. It rendered outstanding counterespionage and intelligence services before and during the second World War, and has been reasonably successful in dealing with Communist and Soviet agents during the present conflict between Russia and the United States.

As a result, the director of the F.B.I. has become an official who is much more powerful, politically, than the Attorney General, while his organization has become the darling of Congress in dealing with "subversive activities." Matters have now reached the stage where, in addition to being nominated by the President and confirmed by the Senate, government officials must also be "cleared" by the F.B.I.

In every other country where a national police organization has achieved comparable powers, it has eventually abused them. The present director is fifty-eight years old and had a distinguished record of service in the Department of Justice before becoming head of the F.B.I. in 1924 as part of the Republican clean-up after the Teapot Dome scandals and the disgrace of Harding's

Attorney General Harry Daugherty of Ohio. Hoover is a fully qualified lawyer and has been careful to insist that his G-men have a thorough knowledge of law as well as judo, gunplay, and modern police technique. Yet Edgar Hoover will not forever remain as the director of the F.B.I.; other less able and less scrupulous men may rise to control this powerful and respected agency, with its thousands of operatives, its vast mysterious files and its growing power to decide who may or may not be considered "loyal" to his own country.

If the cold war should be intensified, that power might become inconsistent with traditional freedom in the United States. The police state has suppressed freedom in other lands and in other eras of history, and we are not immune from history or human nature.

Even if we assume, as most of us do, that our tradition of liberty is too robust to be destroyed by such a process, it remains a fact that, for the duration of the cold war, the F.B.I. is a vital part of our national defense system and, like the armed services, will need wise and firm control by "Ike's" Attorney General.

IX

THE FIGHT FOR THE WATER HOLE

1. POLITICS, POLITICS

A POLITICAL administration can be no stronger than the political party which supports it. If that party loses control of Congress, power to act departs from the executive. That is the basis of our two-party system.

Equally basic is the fact that it is almost as bad for a party to be too long out of power as it is for a party to stay in office too long. The last breeds self-satisfaction and corruption, the first breeds self-distrust and factional bitterness.

No sooner had the votes been counted in "Ike's" landslide victory of November, 1952 than a little cloud no bigger than a politician's mouth appeared on the Republican horizon. Whereas Eisenhower had received over fifty-five per cent. of the popular vote and 442 of the 531 electoral votes, his seven million plurality did not carry over into the Republican Party as a whole. The Senate had been 49-to-47 Democratic; after the election it was

49-to-47 Republican, if you count Wayne Morse of Oregon as a Republican, something to which he loudly objected. In the House of Representatives the Republicans picked up a small working majority of nine votes—221 to 212—but a check of the election returns showed that the Republicans had actually received less than half of all the votes cast for congressmen. While this apparent minority position is due to overwhelming Democratic majorities for congressmen from the southern states, it did not furnish a comfortable or reassuring picture for the Republican Party managers to see that "Ike's" plurality was twice as large as the Republican majorities in contested districts. Put one way, "Ike" led his ticket; stated another way, the Republican Party trailed "Ike" rather badly.

The congressional elections of 1954 could determine whether the Eisenhower administration, like that of Herbert Hoover, would abruptly be shorn of its power to direct national affairs. A Democratic resurgence could deprive the Republicans of control over both branches of Congress and impose frustration on the new Republican President.

Many signs supported the belief that, under normal political trends, this might easily happen. Failure to reduce taxes, a continued drop in farm prices, a serious business recession, a continued stalemate in Korea—any or all of these could disappoint the hopes of the thirty-three million Americans who had trooped to the polls with the cry, "I like Ike!", and lead to a general disillusionment in favor of the Democratic opposition.

So the story of the eighty-third Congress resolves itself into the familiar fight for the water hole or, if more modern imagery is now in order, into a struggle to determine whether the Republicans shall expend their beachhead or be driven back into the sea.

The management of the Republican Party, at this juncture, was a house subdivided against itself. The former national chairman, Arthur E. Summerfield of Michigan, had been named by Eisenhower as Postmaster-General, with control of the most effective political patronage in the country. Truman had rendered Summerfield's task somewhat difficult by "covering into Civil Service" the thousands of Democratic postmasters who had received patronage appointments during the twenty years of Democratic Party control at Washington. So the Republican organization was unable to act promptly and effectively with this important instrument of political power.

Summerfield—according to the Democrats—was a member of the mythical "General Motors dynasty" that was supposed—again according to the Democrats—to have captured the Republican Party. Actually, he was head of the largest Chevrolet sales agency in the world and an independent political power in Michigan. He was born in the little Michigan community of Pinconning fifty-four years ago and, after getting as far as the eighth grade in the public schools of Bay City and Flint, Michigan, had to go to work at the age of thirteen for Weston-Mott, axle manufacturers, later absorbed by General Motors. From there he graduated into the Buick Motor Company and during the first World War worked with the Chevrolet ammunition department. Shortly after the armistice, he decided to go into the real-estate business. In 1924 he became a Michigan oil distributor, and just one month before the Wall Street crash of 1929 started his own Chevrolet agency in Flint and has stayed with it ever since.

Summerfield didn't get into politics until 1943, when he became finance director of the Michigan Republican central committee. He was a successful fund raiser and the following year he was chosen Republican national committeeman from Michigan, a position which he held until he joined "Ike's" Cabinet. This brought him onto the national level of politics and he served as acting chairman of the Republican strategy committee which was organized in 1949, after the '48 disappointment.

He is a joiner in moderation—Masons, Elks, Kiwanis—and a solid citizen who married young, when only nineteen, and has two children. He has also been active in the boys' clubs movement in Michigan, in the National Automobile Dealers Association, and on the Council of Foreign Relations. In short, he is a self-made man who worked his way up to the top of the tree without any favors and few educational advantages.

Summerfield went into the Eisenhower camp at Chicago, after some slick political footwork which drove the "Ike" managers frantic. The Michigan Republicans, with their powerful backing from the automotive industry, held the balance of power between Taft and Eisenhower. Ohio, Indiana, Illinois, and Wisconsin were strongly for Taft. If Summerfield had brought Michigan into the Senator's camp, as he might have done, it would have faced the "Ike-likers" with a solid Midwestern line-up. Summerfield went with the Eisenhower side when he became convinced, as a result of a statewide canvas, district by district, that the voters of Michigan wanted Eisenhower. He had previously had all the candidates speak in Michigan. Taft, in fact, had been there four times. Summerfield joined the Eisenhower side and was made chairman of the Republican National Committee. This was a prudent decision, as it went far to reassure the Taft group in the party that the Deweyites were not in complete control. Summerfield ran the Washington end of the national campaign under considerable difficulties, but with the discovery of the wide gap between "Ike's" political popularity and that of the conservative Republican candidates, a new approach was indicated.

This approach was supplied by Charles Wesley Roberts of Kansas, who was executive director of the national Eisenhower headquarters in Washington during the pre-convention campaign. Summerfield made Wes

Roberts the director of organization for the Republican National Committee.

Unfortunately, it was only an approach, because Roberts felt obliged to resign barely two months after he had undertaken the job. He suffered from two serious disadvantages: not being rich, he had accepted a salary as national chairman, which tended to reduce him to the status of an employee of the committee, and he got caught and smeared in an intra-Republican Party squabble in Kansas. When a committee of the state legislature at Topeka attacked him as a lobbyist on the ground that he had accepted a sizable public-relations fee for helping arrange the sale of a private hospital to the state, he decided to step out of the chairmanship. This incident deprived the Eisenhower administration of a man who was almost uniquely qualified to maintain the volunteer enthusiasm which had won the election for the New Republicans.

He was promptly replaced as national chairman by Leonard Wood Hall, who was born in Teddy Roosevelt's home town of Oyster Bay, Long Island, in 1900, and named after Teddy's famous superior officer in the Roughriders, Colonel Leonard Wood. Hall's career has been publicly undramatic and politically significant: a law degree from Georgetown University and a practicing lawyer since he was 21 years old; three terms in the New York state legislature; a three-year term as sheriff of Nassau County, New York; election to Congress in

1938; fourteen years in the House of Representatives, ending in his appointment to the delectable office of Surrogate of Nassau County.

So much for the bare facts; now for the truth behind them. Len Hall—bald, clean-shaven, with horn-rimmed spectacles and a firm jaw—is one of the ablest political technicians in Republican national politics. He handled the Congressional end of the 1952 campaign for Eisenhower and turned in an energetic performance which resulted in a slim but sufficient Republican majority in the House of Representatives along with the Eisenhower landslide. Hall had wished to be named Republican national committeeman from New York, but the post was already very competently filled by J. Russel Sprague, also of Nassau County; Hall was therefore made Surrogate, pending future developments. His name was advanced for the national chairmanship by Speaker of the House Joe Martin of Massachusetts, and was backed by other national Republicans before the Dewey organization also came to Hall's support.

He lacks Wes Roberts' flair for enlisting the enthusiastic support of liberals and independents, but he is widely known and liked by Republican politicians throughout the country. He is also a first-class political practitioner in a job which could be bungled by inexpert management. He will have the good will of the regular Republican organizations throughout the country and the full approval of the Republicans in Congress. His chief danger is that he may be, as are many professional politicians, disposed to discount the importance and good will of the six million independent voters without regular political affiliations whose support can elect Presidents and whose indifference can destroy national administrations.

2. "Poor Richard"

The spearhead of the Republican political drive on Capitol Hill is the man who is separated by a single heartbeat from the Presidency of the United States: Vice-President Richard Nixon.

Dick Nixon is one of the youngest men to occupy this post, being barely forty years old, and his Vice-Presidential candidacy occasioned more controversy and misgivings than any in our history. He is dark-haired, serious, energetic, and self-confident, and first achieved national fame for his part in exposing Alger Hiss on the House Un-American Affairs Committee in 1948.

He was the unanimous choice of a committee of thirty-two Republican leaders, after four hours of deliberation, as "Ike's" running-mate in the 1952 campaign. A young war veteran with a good record, personable and progressive, Nixon was acceptable to all the factions of the party. He had shown a genuine understanding of the world problem; he had given an exhibition of skill, restraint, and persistence in the exposure of Alger Hiss, winning the commendation of both pro- and anti-Communists; he was admired by individuals as diverse as Irving Ives and Robert Taft. His greatest opposition, in fact, came from Governor Earl Warren of California, who was far from pleased by the selection of Nixon for Vice-President and remained so until the eve of the election. Warren was an avowed candidate for the Presidential nomination and the old New York–California axis established by Dewey in 1948 had been shaken by Warren's failure to realize in time that "Ike's" candidacy had become a bandwagon. Nixon had urged Warren to relax and enjoy the inevitable, but the governor was stubborn and met with unnecessary disappointment.

Nixon's past career had given little indication that he was of national stature. He was a very normal sort of young California war veteran, born of Quaker parents in the little town of Yerba Linda, and brought up in the Quaker tradition of thrift, faith, and hard work. He went to the public schools and delivered groceries and worked at filling stations after school hours to earn money. He went on to attend Whittier College in Whittier, California, where he developed into a successful debater and played football, although never making the 'varsity. On graduation, he received a scholarship to study at Duke University Law School. With his law degree, he returned to enter a law firm at Whittier and five years later was just beginning to build up a practice when Pearl Harbor altered all his personal plans.

Those plans included his family life, for in 1940 he had

met and married pretty Patricia Ryan, a Nevada girl of
his own age who was teaching classes in typing and shorthand at the local high school. When war came, Nixon
promptly joined the navy and went on to serve in the
South Pacific, winning two battle stars and two special
commendations—nothing very dramatic but a good testi-
monial to courage and character.

After V-J Day, he returned to Whittier, re-estab-
lished his home, and started to make up for the four years
of lost time. He wasn't allowed to do so. A citizens committee in the old 12th Congressional district of California
urged him to run for Congress in 1946 against the entrenched five-term New Deal Democrat, Jerry Voorhis.
In that year of meat shortages and "Had enough?",
Nixon won the seat and was re-elected two years later.
In 1950, a similar group of California citizens urged him
to run for the Senate against another New Deal Democrat, Helen Gahagan Douglas. Again Nixon was successful, winning the senatorship with the overwhelming majority of more than seven hundred thousand votes.

In the meantime, trouble was brewing for "Poor Richard." As a poor man, he lacked the personal fortune necessary to finance the political end of a senatorship from a
large state such as California. Accordingly, his friends
set up a special fund under independent audit and control to defray such expenses as mailing, printing, travel,
and entertainment. As a conspicuous opponent of Communism in the matter of Alger Hiss and as the man who

had defeated two prominent New Deal Democrats, his support inevitably came from conservative business interests in Southern California, chiefly those in oil and real estate.

In the middle of the Presidential campaign, the Democrats exploded their giant cracker. The Nixon fund was "exposed" and the impression was piously given that Senator Nixon had been bribed by "selfish corporate interests" to serve their private profit at the expense of the public. The "scandal" was well-timed and the Republicans were flabbergasted, as the Democratic smear-picture was far out of harmony with "Ike's" crusade for honesty in government. Many upper-bracket Republicans argued that "Ike" should dismiss Nixon from the ticket like a clumsy butler. Others argued that this would be fatal to the party's success. Senator Taft and Governor Dewey, like two estranged parents hovering at the bedside of a sick child, both urged Eisenhower to stand by Nixon. And on the Nixon train, Bill Rogers communicated with his law partner, Jack Wells, who was working with Dewey in New York, to give Nixon time to present his defense.

Actually, the "scandal" proved to be the turning point in the campaign. Nixon's nationwide telecast from Los Angeles, with his pretty wife paralyzed with nervousness at his side, and his account of his personal finances, his wife and children, and the dog "Checkers," was denounced as "soap opera" by the disgruntled Democrats.

But it more than made the case for the propriety of the Nixon fund. Women wept as they watched the television screen, and one man at Dewey headquarters said somberly: "When he came to talk about his financial problems, I almost cried myself; they were so like my own!" Governor Stevenson of Illinois was revealed to have administered not one, but three, similar funds on his own behalf, and was never able to recapture full public attention after the failure of the Nixon smear.

Some time after the election it was discovered that the Democrats had also prepared elaborate forgeries as a follow-up charge against the Republican Vice-Presidential nominee and the whole episode boomeranged in a sharp reminder that bad morals, like bad manners, are also very bad politics.

Under the Constitution of the United States, Dick Nixon is the man who will become President if Eisenhower should be unable to perform his duties. Three times in the present century, a Vice-President has become our chief executive as a result of the death of the President of the United States: "Teddy" Roosevelt after McKinley's assassination, Calvin Coolidge after Harding contracted ptomaine poisoning in Alaska, and Harry Truman after F.D.R. died of a cerebral hemorrhage at Warm Springs, Georgia. "Teddy" and "Cautious Cal" were distinct improvements over their predecessors, Truman a costly anticlimax. What qualities which might become of national and world importance does Nixon possess?

On the record, Nixon is a Quaker, very much in earnest, but humorous, an advocate of social advances in the teeth of the intense conservatism of many California Republicans. He lacks wide experience of the world outside the United States or deep familiarity with national affairs. He is dependable, loyal, hard-working, honest, and a little brash.

But his wife, Pat Nixon, is evidence that this deadly serious young lawyer is the kind of man most Americans like and trust. She is not only pretty and the mother of two pretty little girls; she is the self-reliant kind of business girl who is typical of millions of other American women who earn their living. She worked her way through the University of Southern California by doing research, grading papers, and acting as sales clerk in department stores on Saturdays and during her vacations. Before that, in order to accumulate money for her college course, she had worked as an x-ray technician in New York City and, after her graduation in 1937, supported herself by teaching typing, shorthand, and commercial practice at the Whittier High School.

During the war, until her husband was assigned to sea duty with the Pacific Fleet, she followed him around from one naval establishment to the next in order to be with him, and supported herself at various jobs in the various places he was assigned, once as a teller in a local bank and again as a research worker on a government project. In Congress she acted as his secretary without drawing the salary the job rated. Slightly built—she is only five foot five and tips the scales at 110 pounds—and with reddish blonde hair, she is decorative as well as smart and useful. Most Americans who have seen her, as millions did during the campaign on television, will conclude that if a woman like that admires and respects a man, that man must be absolutely straight and dependable.

3. Messrs. Republicans

Part of the inevitable price paid by the Republicans for being out of power too long was that party leadership in Congress automatically gravitated to men from "sure" Republican states and congressional districts. Such "sure" constituencies were so congenitally G.O.P. that there was a premium on stand-pat conformity and a tendency to regard Republicanism as a religion with rigid articles of faith.

Men of this conservatism are needed to prevent the party from becoming nothing but a receptacle for opportunists and expedients, but when they dominate its counsels they tend to make policy a matter of official party dogma rather than trust to events, experiment, and public opinion to determine their course of action.

The great protagonist of this process during the twenty years in the Democratic wilderness was Ohio's

Senator Robert A. Taft, "Mr. Republican," the thrice-defeated contender for his party's Presidential nomination. If Taft rather than Willkie had been nominated in 1940, his friends believe it is possible he might have won because Taft favored staying out of World War II and would have run on a straightforward peace policy. If Taft rather than Dewey had been nominated in 1948, there are many Republicans who insist that Taft would almost certainly have beaten Truman in the Presidential contest. But if Taft, rather than Eisenhower, had won the 1952 nomination, there was not a single major Republican leader outside the Middle West who would have bet a plugged nickel on Taft to defeat Adlai Stevenson.

What kind of a man is it who can command such fanatical loyalties and arouse such bitter opposition as this sixty-four-year-old son of the good old President and Chief Justice William Howard Taft? "Bob" Taft is one of the most honest, dependable, and intelligent men in public life. He is also one of the most irritating and unimaginative politicians in the history of the Republican Party.

His capacity to exasperate was first formalized when his easygoing father, who had married the brilliant and strong-minded Helen Herron, exclaimed in the course of an argument with his eldest son: "If I had never set eyes on you in my life and met you in the middle of the Gobi Desert, I'd say: 'There's a child of Nelly Herron!' "

The former President was not the first or last parent to

be provoked by the practical side of genetics, but it is notable among those who know the family that, whereas Bob's brother Charlie is well-known for his pronounced religious activities, Bob is the man to whom people always turn for help in time of trouble. He was born to wealth and political privilege in Cincinnati in 1889, attended his Uncle Horace's Taft School in Connecticut, graduated from Yale in 1910, and received his Harvard law degree in 1913. These dates are important, for they mean that Taft's whole character and outlook were formed when the Republican Party had been secure in the saddle for fifty years and when the world as a whole had prospered under the *Pax Brittanica* for nearly a century. To call a man an isolationist because he honestly prefers such a state of affairs to the present world confusion is scarcely fair to him or to history. But to believe we can turn back the page of history is scarcely fair to the rest of the world, which knows it can't be done.

Bob Taft's career followed the lines predestined for one born to Republican wealth and privilege in the days before the two world wars. He practiced law; he began a lifelong devotion the year after he got his law degree by marrying Martha Bowers, still his wife and the mother of his four sons. During the first war he worked with Herbert Hoover in the United States Food Administration and later in the American Relief Administration in Europe. Shortly after Ohio elected its last President, in 1920, "Bob" Taft went into Ohio politics. He served five years in the state legislature, ending as speaker of the house in 1926. He also served a term in the state senate and was elected to the United States Senate in 1938, the year which witnessed the first major political reaction against Roosevelt. Since then he has been re-elected to two additional six-year terms and has made himself both feared and respected in Congress.

Taft is a baffling mixture of conservatism and liberalism, of high moral courage and a numbing lack of moral imagination. During the Republican 80th Congress, he served on the Senate Labor Committee and sponsored liberal measures for public housing and education. He also sponsored the Taft-Hartley Labor-Management Relations Law. He dared to speak out boldly, and alone, in protest against the kangaroo-court legal lynching of the German war criminals at a time when most public men preferred to close their eyes to the judicial murder of foreign leaders for having lost the war. He was branded as an enemy of labor, yet he single-handedly blocked Truman's fascistic proposal to draft the railway workers into the army in order to break the strike in 1946. Yet he could not see why he should refuse to benefit by the "theft" of the Texas delegates to the 1952 Convention, even after he was reminded how his father lost in 1912 because "Teddy" Roosevelt had charged a similar Taft "theft" of southern delegates. He is a smiling, flat-voiced man with a tart tongue. He makes needless enemies, is apt to talk too much and too soon, and is also able to change his position swiftly and gracefully if he finds himself mistaken or misinformed.

His failure to win the 1952 Republican nomination threatened for a time to cost "Ike" the election. Taft's supporters were deeply, in fact religiously, loyal to "Mr. Republican" and harbored fierce resentment against the Eisenhower forces. It was only after the legendary "Surrender of Morningside Heights," when "Ike" and Taft made a public parade of harmony during the campaign, that the Senator persuaded his followers to throw their strength behind the Republican national ticket. Taft himself campaigned vigorously across the nation for "Ike," and a fair share of the credit for Eisenhower's victory must go to the good sportsmanship of the man whom "Ike" defeated at Chicago after the bitterest Republican convention contest in forty years.

Washington newspapermen confidently predict that Taft will sooner or later break with the Eisenhower administration, but Washington newspapermen, collectively, have never yet been right. "Bob" Taft has personally abandoned all Presidential ambitions and has every motive to make a success of his party's return to power. The chances are that he will remain absolutely loyal to the President, although differing with him strongly on many issues, unless faced with a real nationwide revolt of the conservative Republicans. These he must follow, because he is their leader.

Although the conservative Old Guard wing of the

party was badly damaged in the 1952 election, it still contains able and powerful leaders, of whom perhaps the most influential, next to Taft, is Senator Eugene D. Millikin of Colorado, chairman of the Senate Finance Committee. Millikin is a large, good-natured, studious man of sixty-two who was born in Hamilton, Ohio, but whose parents moved to the Silver State at a time when it was one of Wall Street's most prosperous colonies, a virtual satrapy of the Rockefeller coal-and-iron interests. He graduated from the University of Chicago Law School the same year that Taft obtained his Harvard law degree and two years later popped up in Colorado politics as Governor Carlson's executive secretary. When we entered the first World War, Millikin promptly enlisted as a private in the Colorado National Guard and served with the infantry in France and with the army of occupation in Germany, ending up as lieutenant-colonel of engineers with a citation for distinguished service from General Pershing.

Back home in Denver, he engaged in business and law practice with former Colorado Senator Schuyler from 1919 to 1933, and later married the Senator's widow. In 1941, following the death of Senator Alva Adams, the Governor of Colorado appointed Millikin to fill the vacancy in the Senate. Millikin was elected in his own right in 1942, re-elected in 1944 and again in 1950. He is an expert on banking, currency, and fiscal policy, an undramatic, likable bruin of a straightforward conservative. He can be relied upon not to rock the Republican boat.

More dramatic and less dependable, from the administration viewpoint, is "Bertie" McCormick's Senator from Illinois, Everett McKinley Dirksen, chairman of the Republican Senate Campaign Committee and one of the party's ablest speakers. Dirksen was born in Pekin, Illinois, in 1896, and received a law degree from the University of Minnesota. He married a home-town girl, Louella Carver of Pekin, and was all set to practice law and support his family when the bugles sounded for World War I. Like Adams, he promptly enlisted as a private and was promoted from the ranks to corporal, to sergeant, and finally to second lieutenant in the course of eighteen months' service overseas with the 328th Field Artillery, the 19th Balloon Company, and general staff intelligence. After the war he dropped law and went into business as a draining and dredging contractor, as manufacturer of electric washing machines and as co-owner of a wholesale bakery in Pekin.

His business success led to city politics. In 1926 he was elected commissioner of finance of Pekin for a four-year term. After losing a primary fight for Congress in 1930, he was elected to the House of Representatives in 1932 and served there continuously until 1949, when he retired voluntarily. In 1950 he ran for the Senate and was elected with a majority of two hundred and ninety thousand votes over Democratic Senate Majority Leader '

Scott Lucas, with an assist from "Joe" McCarthy. During this same period he became increasingly active in Republican national affairs, at conventions, on the party's policy committee, and as a campaigner.

Dirksen was the man designated to do the hatchet job on Governor Dewey at the 1952 Republican Convention, and his speech rates as a piece of masterly insult and polished impertinence. To the delighted whoops of the packed galleries, he chided and rebuked the leader of the Eisenhower forces in terms which bit like hydrochloric acid. Dewey simply went out and had his shoes shined, and with "Ike's" nomination, the incident passed down the drain, where it belonged. But Dirksen is still a vigorous man of fifty-six, with ambition, organizing ability, a thick skin, and a sound digestion. If Dirksen's friend and ally, the formidable publisher of the Chicago *Tribune*, should decide to expel the Eisenhower administration from the Republican party, it is likely that Everett Dirksen, rather than Robert Alphonso Taft, will be the leader of the secession.

4. WAYNE MORSE AND "JOE" McCARTHY

The chief opposition that Eisenhower faces for the present within his own party comes from two mutually exclusive Senators, one a crypto-Democrat and one a former Democrat—Wayne Morse of Oregon and "Joe" McCarthy of Wisconsin.

Morse has staked his convictions and career on the theory that Eisenhower has surrendered to reactionary political and industrial interests, that no good fruit can come from any tree watered by Senator Taft, and that by 1960 or even by 1956 there will be a sharply radical change in the political climate. Stated another way, Morse is gambling that there will be peace, not war, with Russia and that the Eisenhower administration will bungle the economic and social readjustments which must follow any extensive industrial demobilization.

Self-righteous, contentious, and more than a little unhappy in his present lonely political position, Wayne Morse is a man of deep convictions and great personal charm. He is dark-haired and dark-moustached, lean and wiry, looking a bit like a Mississippi steamboat gambler who has acquired religion, and is possessed of a fine legal brain and a skill in parliamentary debate which are being wasted by his self-imposed isolation, high and very dry between the two evenly divided parties in the Senate.

Wayne Lyman Morse was born of Baptist New England parents on a farm near Madison, Wisconsin in 1900. At the University of Wisconsin he shone as a debater and went on after graduation to take a job as debating instructor at the University of Minnesota, where Harold Stassen was one of his students. Even after receiving his Minnesota law degree in 1924, Morse continued to take an interest in debating, first as a young law professor and then as dean of the law school at the University of Oregon. As a matter of fact, he nearly debated himself out of his teaching job as a result of the skill and power with which he argued against an officially approved merger of the university with Oregon State College.

In Oregon he also became so deeply interested in the theory and practice of labor arbitration that he was eventually appointed to the War Labor Board in 1942. During the war, Morse dared to lock horns with Secretary of the Interior Harold Ickes when the latter broke the War Labor Board's wage formula in favor of John L. Lewis's United Mine Workers. Ickes got the coal without a strike but Morse saved his administrative soul, and Roosevelt encouraged the contentious young Oregonian to go into politics rather than remain in the executive branch of government. Oregon is staunch Republican territory and in 1944, when the veteran Senate Minority Leader, Charles McNary of Oregon, died in office, the governor naturally appointed a conservative Republican, Guy Cordon, to fill the vacancy. But Oregon is also progressive-minded, so F.D.R. sent word to the New Deal Democrats to pitch in and vote for Morse in the Republican primary. They did and Morse won the primary, like the regular election, with the help of the Democratic administration. Six years later, in 1950, he was again elected, once more largely with the help of Democratic and labor votes, this time with the largest majority in Oregon's history.

Before then, Morse had made his conscience sharply

felt in national politics. In 1948, he broke with Harold Stassen and favored the nomination of Senator Arthur Vandenberg of Michigan in 1948, partly because he believed Vandenberg's leadership was needed to unite the party and also—and this is pure Wayne Morse—in order to lead the Republican party away from control by the Taft "reactionary wing."

Since then, Morse had tended to take his own position entirely from Taft. Whatever Taft is for, Morse is against; wherever Taft feels at home, Morse suffers an attack of political claustrophobia. His break with Eisenhower in 1952 followed this too simple substitute for political self-examination.

Even before the Republican Convention Morse had been miffed when Henry Cabot Lodge of Massachusetts bustled into Oregon before the primary and tried to take the leadership of the Oregon Eisenhower delegates away from Morse, although the latter had been one of the first Eisenhower supporters on the floor of the Senate. Then on his return home from a quick inspection of American military bases in Europe Morse read in the newspapers about the "Surrender of Morningside Heights." This conference between Senator Taft and General Eisenhower was a bitter blow to a man who had consistently opposed the "reactionary wing" of the G.O.P. for nearly eight years in the Senate; when it was announced that "Ike" and Taft were in over-all agreement on labor policy, Morse simply went wild.

He acted with less than his usual clearheadedness. Two serious accidents with horses had left him weak and in constant pain, and he swiftly painted himself into a home-made suit of tar and feathers. First he announced that he could not support "Ike" but that, as an elected Republican, he had no moral right to support "Ike's" Democratic opponent. Then two weeks later, he came out in support of Stevenson and spoke for him. There were rumors that Truman had promised to make Morse Attorney General and the President had, in fact, already given Morse's private secretary a post on the Labor Relations Board, but it would be completely unfair to conclude that Morse was seduced by Democratic patronage. He fell from Republican virtue, but in his own time. After the election, he refused to congratulate the winner or to seek reconciliation with the party he had abandoned. He told both Republicans and Democrats that he wanted no Senate committee assignments from either party and then was outraged when he lost his post on the committees which deal with defense and labor matters. His role in the Senate became one of niggling nuisance, as when he blocked confirmation of Eisenhower's Cabinet officers on inauguration day on the ground that he had not studied the committee hearings on the individuals.

He has become bitter and still lacks the great cause which could dramatize and utilize his lonely eminence as one man in the Senate who could dare to speak the truth, since he has no party to consider and no career to be served. He tells his friends that he expects to be defeated in 1956 by the angry Oregon Republicans who rewarded his "ratting" in the campaign by sending him a pair of gold cufflinks in symbolic similitude of an equine posterior.

At forty-four, Joseph R. McCarthy is just about as far to the right of Wayne Morse as a man can be and still stay inside the solar system, let alone the Republican Party. He comes uncomfortably close to being what Henry A. Wallace used to call "the common man." He is, in fact, the kind of man who commonly comes to the top in periods of turmoil. He is tough, shrewd, and so controversial a public figure that to most Americans he is either saint or devil, never an ordinary hard-hitting self-made Irish lawyer from the cutover lands of Wisconsin. Well-built, dark-haired, clean-shaven, he has the smooth face of an actor.

And he has staged an impressive act. As wartime differences of opinion hardened into postwar conflicts of policy between Washington and Moscow, "Joe" McCarthy had his chance at the Big Time. He moved right out on the stage of the American Communist drama and has made a political career of exposing Soviet spies, Communist sympathizers, loyalty risks, security risks, and sexual deviates in the State Department.

McCarthy's own explanation of the violent antagonism he has aroused is contained in the statement he made in numerous campaign speeches in Wisconsin: When he was a boy on a farm in Wisconsin his mother kept chickens; every now and then a skunk got into the henhouse and started to kill the poultry; so somebody had to go in and kill the skunk; for some time afterwards, McCarthy explained, whoever had done that necessary job wasn't very popular in his mother's kitchen.

He first came on the scene in 1909, as one of a large family of children born to poor Irish Catholic parents on a farm in Appleton, Wisconsin. He had a hard life. He got as far as the eighth grade in the public school, and then had to go to work in a grocery. In order to qualify to study law at Marquette University, he completed a four-year high school course in a single year when he was already twenty. He supported himself at law school by giving boxing lessons. As a poor lawyer and a Democrat, he ran against the local Republican judge in 1939 and was triumphantly elected circuit judge at the age of thirty. He was re-elected in 1945, without opposition, while absent on service in the Pacific with the Marine Corps. He had enlisted in June of 1942, and spent two and a half years on active duty in the Marine Corps air branch. He was a good fighter and earned citations for bravery.

In the meantime, unlike most Irish Democrats, he had switched sides in politics, joined the Republicans and made a try for the G.O.P. Senate nomination from Wisconsin in 1944, but was passed over in favor of the incumbent, Alexander Wiley. Two years later his time had come, and at the Oshkosh convention of the Wisconsin Republicans he beat the late Senator "Bob" La-Follette for the nomination.

In Washington he soon received what was usually considered the accolade for integrity, the wrath of the Truman administration. After he had made wild charges in a radio speech about the number of Communists in the State Department, suave Democratic Senator Millard Tydings of Maryland leisurely undertook to deal with "Joe" McCarthy. When the smoke had cleared away after the 1950 elections, Tydings was no longer a Senator, and other Democrats who had supported him in the attack on McCarthy had also been beaten, like Scott Lucas in Illinois, or were clearly doomed to defeat, like "Bill" Benton of Connecticut.

At this point, the Democrats decided that McCarthy was worse than a nuisance; he became a "national menace" or, better still, an effective campaign issue against the Republicans. It was a good idea but it didn't work.

In retrospect, it can fairly be said that "Joe" McCarthy, whatever his methods and his motives, rendered a service to the country in dramatizing a state of affairs which could be extremely dangerous to our survival in case of war with the Soviet empire. The Truman administration, not unnaturally, tried to minimize the damaging facts and spoke loftily about "red herrings," but mousetrapped itself when both the Alger Hiss case and the election returns showed that Senator McCarthy was not barking down a political posthole.

McCarthy's role in the 1952 campaign was a reminder that nothing builds up a western Senator so much as to be attacked by eastern newspapers and politicians. He won renomination and re-election to the Senate without much difficulty, although running well behind Eisenhower in Wisconsin. Under "Ike," he continued to jab and nag at the State Department, his pet target, and to act as final authority on who was fit and proper to serve American diplomacy. In attacking "Ike's" approved choice for American Ambassador to Moscow, because Bohlen had been at the Yalta Conference, McCarthy edged onto the same lonely ground occupied by Wayne Morse of Oregon, since "Ike" can command the overwhelming support of the Democrats, in addition to most of the Republicans, whenever he finds it necessary to overrule McCarthy and his Democratic Yalta Ego, Pat McCarran of Nevada.

If, as many Americans believe, there is an irrepressible conflict between America and Russia, McCarthy seems to have chosen his ground more wisely than has Wayne Morse. Even if peace should break out, he can take comfort in the career of Congressman Hamilton Fish of New York, who also exploited the anti-Communist issue in the 1920's. Fish survived politically the whole period of Soviet-American friendship and it was not until 1942, when Russia was actually our ally against the Axis, that Dewey encompassed his defeat.

Morse has no such prospect. Even if peace should be restored he has failed to appreciate the fact that there may be no automatic economic depression to give point to his warnings. Yet he, like McCarthy, represents the extremes of policy between which the Eisenhower administration and the New Republicans must steer a middle course.

5. Two Loyal Oppositions

This course is made much easier by the fact that there are two "loyal oppositions" in Congress—the two Democratic parties, north and south.

The ivy has begun to grow over the bitter feud between Progressive and Old Guard Republicans in the forty years which have passed since the Taft-Roosevelt rift of 1912, but moss, blasted oaks, and owls' nests line both sides of the deep Mason-Dixiecrat chasm which divides the twenty-two Senators of the Solid South from the twenty-five Democrats of the northern and Border states. These two halves of the Democratic donkey were stitched together by jobs and subsidies and a lot of soft soap under Roosevelt and Truman, but the deep difference of their interests, policies, and philosophies of government led to the ominous Dixiecrat breakaway of 1948 and the wave of southern votes for Eisenhower four years later.

By an odd coincidence, the Solid Southerners—with their deep Colonial roots—are closer biologically if not logically to the New Republicans than to the northern Democrats. And the northern Democrats, with their industrial interests and multi-racial electorates, are closer philosophically to the New Republicans than they are to the Congressional representatives of the one-party system of the Solid South.

This Democratic division means that Eisenhower can count on not one but two loyal oppositions and that he is likely to command at least half of the Democratic votes in Congress on any issue, conservative or progressive, which he may advocate as the policy of his administration. This fact somewhat dims the hopes, in advance, of any conceivable Old Guard Republican revolt against "Ike's" leadership. The divided Democrats guarantee the New Republicans more freedom of action in the 83rd Congress than the actual party division indicates.

The leaders of the southern Democratic Party in Congress are able, plausible, and attractive men. In previous Congresses they have tended to co-operate with the Old Guard wing of the Republican Party and have repeatedly applied a legislative brake to New Deal legislation.

Possibly the most respected of them all is sixty-six-year-old Senator Harry Flood Byrd of Virginia. Byrd, with the late Carter Glass (who in his latter days imagined he had invented the Federal Reserve System), has been the fiscal conscience of his party for the last twenty years.

His political career began, quietly enough, with his ten years' presidency of the Shenandoah Valley Turnpike Company from 1908 to 1918. His interest in good roads, like his advocacy of the "pay-as-you-go" principle in government, won him election to the Virginia state senate in 1915. In 1926 he was granted a four-year term as Governor of Virginia and he was a remarkably good one, deserving credit he has never received from vociferous northern "liberals" for his Anti-Mob Violence Law of 1928—a measure which put a complete stop to lynchings in the Old Dominion from that day to this.

Byrd maintained his technical political virginity during the Eisenhower campaign with an all but metaphysical adroitness, but was known to favor "Ike" and have endearing young qualms about Adlai, so his state dutifully voted Republican for the first time since 1928. Byrd was also personally responsible for calling to Eisenhower's attention the hellish fact that Charles Wilson's holdings of General Motors stock would constitute a "conflict of interest" in the latter's post as Secretary of Defense.

Of greater individual charm and personal legislative ability than Byrd, though scarcely Byrd's match as a political power, is Senator Richard Brevard Russell of Georgia. Like Byrd, Russell is of old English Colonial ancestry, but is more of a southern senator's senator than is Byrd and shines in committee work and as general manager of the southern Democratic Party in Congress. Tall, pleasant, easy-mannered and extremely adroit, "Dick" Russell made himself the leader of the southern forces opposed to the nomination of either Estes Kefauver or Harry Truman in 1952. He stayed with the party during the Presidential campaign, not too vigorously, and saw that his state turned in a conventional Georgia majority for the Democratic national candidates.

Russell was born in the little Barrow County town of Winder, Georgia, in 1897 and is a fair representative of the New South which grew up after the Spanish-American war. That South has thrown off the Ku Klux Klan infection and is slowly adjusting itself to labor unions and similar phenomena of the industrial age.

There is a still newer South than the agrarian Dixie of Harry Byrd and Dick Russell, and that is the industrial South which is rising in such states as Alabama and Tennessee, and which came of age under the New Deal. That South is represented by Senator John Sparkman of Alabama, his party's candidate for Vice-President in the 1952 political barbecue.

Sparkman was one of the eleven children of a poor sharecropper in the Alabama hill country. He was born in 1899, had to walk six miles a day to the local Morgan County school, and somehow managed to scrape together seventy five dollars to send himself to the University of Alabama at Tuscaloosa in 1917; he worked his way through college.

After getting his law degree in 1923, he moved to Huntsville, Alabama, where he entered a law firm in 1925 and combined the Siamese-twin practice of southern law and Democratic politics so successfully that he was elected to Congress in 1936. He served five useful and undistinguished terms in the House of Representatives and then, when old Senator John Bankhead, uncle of Tallulah, died, went to the Senate in his place. Two years later he was automatically re-elected to the Senate and will stay there more or less forever, as do most professional politicians from the Deep South.

Sparkman's record in national politics is that of a man who is as liberal as his Alabama constituents allow a man to be and as non-partisan as a southern Democrat allows himself to be.

Men like Byrd, Russell, and Sparkman can be relied upon to support the Eisenhower administration on most foreign-policy issues and on all policies which represent the conservative preference for allowing local authority and individual initiative a fair place in the scheme of things.

By contrast, the northern Democrats are the product of a genuine two-party system of politics. Except for three or four kept Senators who represent special labor or gambling interests, they have to face a large, critical, and mixed general electorate at regular intervals. Frequently they owe their election to public revolt against standpat Republican policies and candidates. Hence they tend to be more articulate and infinitely more progressive than the average southern Democrat. President Eisenhower can count on them to support his leadership on any issue which is in harmony with progressive political principles, since they are New Republicans in all but name. With the collapse of organized labor as the dominant political power in the industrial states, the average liberal Democrat of the North has nowhere to go but the White House.

Consider the representative case of Senator Guy Mark Gillette of Iowa. Guy Gillette, is, for all practical purposes, a progressive Prairie Republican who just happens to wear the Democratic label. He was born in the small town of Cherokee, in northwest Iowa, sixty-four years ago, nine years after his father, of old English and French Huguenot New England ancestry, took up a farm in the country. He fits the prevailing New Republican climate in other respects, too. He is a devout Presbyterian, a Mason, and has always been elected with the help of Republican votes.

Gillette's career has also been typical of the New Republicans. He went to the Cherokee High School and then obtained his law degree from Drake University at Des Moines in 1900, was admitted to the Iowa bar, and returned to practice law in his home town. Before that he had enlisted at the age of fourteen in the Iowa National

Guard and served in the Spanish-American war. He also tried to enlist in the Boer Army in the South African war but was prevented by the State Department's unsympathetic interpretation of the neutrality laws. Gillette was a Democrat in a ninety-six-per-cent. Republican community but in 1907 was elected as Cherokee County prosecutor and in 1912 was sent to the Iowa state senate for a four-year term. When America entered World War I, he promptly enlisted in the army and served as an infantry captain. Incidentally, his brother Claude became an admiral in the United States Navy. In 1932, with the New Deal sweep, he was elected to Congress and re-elected in 1934. Two years after that, Gillette decided to run for the Senate and won in that year of Roosevelt's forty-six-state landslide. In 1938, he was elected for the full six-year term but was beaten in 1944. Four years later he ran once more for the Senate and won by the largest majority in the history of Iowa politics.

Gillette's record is not particularly partisan. He is a steady, calm, level-headed man of deep integrity who survived Roosevelt's attempt to "purge" him in 1938. He refused Truman's offer of a judgeship on the United States Customs Court for the unusual reason that he did not know anything about customs law.

Eisenhower can count on moderate Democrats like Guy Gillette to follow their convictions and give him their support, without regard to party labels, whenever they believe the President is right.

This is equally true of intellectual Democratic leaders such as Senator Paul H. Douglas of Illinois. Douglas is conscientious, emotional, exceedingly intelligent, and, like Gillette, owes his seat in the Senate to many thousands of Republican protest votes which in his case were cast against the corrupt Republican political machine in Illinois.

Paul Douglas is, in fact, a sort of Tom Dewey in reverse. Dewey was born in Michigan and moved east. Douglas was born in New England—at Salem, Massachusetts—and moved west. He spent his boyhood on a primitive farm in northern Maine and worked his way through Bowdoin College by waiting on tables, mixing concrete, handling baggage at the local depot, and selling gelatin desserts. He also found time to play center on the Bowdoin football team and graduated, Phi Beta Kappa, in 1913, when he was barely twenty-one.

After becoming Professor of Industrial Relations at Chicago University in 1923, his work as an economic and political thinker, author, and legislative draftsman won him a national reputation. In the 1930's he helped Democratic Governor Horner bring Illinois up-to-date on such matters as utilities legislation and old-age pensions. He also helped draft the monstrously complicated Federal Security Act.

When we entered the second World War he enlisted as a fifty-year-old private in the Marine Corps. After basic training he was assigned to combat duty in the Pacific. He was wounded at Peleliu, receiving a bronze star for heroism in action, and was wounded a second time, very seriously, at Okinawa. After fourteen months in the hospital he was discharged in 1946 with the rank of lieutenant-colonel.

Two years later, like Guy Gillette, Douglas incurred Truman's jealous enmity by being elected to the Senate from Illinois by a majority of over four hundred thousand votes, whereas the President scraped through by the pitifully small margin of thirty thousand votes in the huge Illinois electorate. Much of the Democratic Party history of the second Truman administration revolved around Douglas' bold fight to keep his campaign promises and the Democratic President's attempt to mow him down. Douglas fought and won his battle to prevent the White House from pocketing the Federal judiciary in Chicago. He was largely responsible for forcing the administration to permit the Federal Reserve Board to perform its duty to check inflationary credit in 1951. He argued, unsuccessfully, for economy in appropriations, including overlavish defense funds, and sponsored, with equal lack of success, intelligent amendments to the Taft-Hartley law. His Senate record was so brilliant and independent that, for a time, he appeared the ablest Presidential candidate his party could nominate. But he would never permit his name to be considered.

So Paul Douglas is another of those northern Democrats upon whom Eisenhower can rely for thick-and-thin support for all measures on the plane of national honor and interest in foreign affairs and of rational progress in domestic issues. He will continue to follow his own conscience in voting, but those who have observed a good New England conscience in action believe that, when the chips are down, Paul Douglas may prove to be a better Eisenhower Republican than many who bear the name and reputation of Republican.

In any case, it is important to note that the election returns of 1948, like those of 1952, show the strength of independent and progressive opinion in American public life, since the liberal Democrats ran embarrassingly far ahead of Truman in 1948. This lends point to the corresponding Old Guard-Progressive cleavage in Republican ranks.

6. THE MIDDLE WAY

The political future lies with the progressive Republicans, regardless of the apparent conservative strength in Congress. Conservative Republican leadership dominates the House of Representatives, as well as the Senate, through seniority and committee chairmanships which go to Congressmen from "sure" Republican districts. But since the more representative electorates are to be found in the large industrial states, taken as a whole, and not in isolated one-hundred-per-cent. G.O.P. bailiwicks, it is easier and more instructive to trace their impact in the Senate than in the House. For example, while Speaker

Joseph Martin has been elected to Congress from Massachusetts almost since the memory of man, Massachusetts as a whole has shifted from Republican to Democratic and back again.

The brutal fact is that the conservative wing of the Republican Party was badly hurt in the 1952 election, while the progressive wing made a powerful showing. Old Guard Republican Senators were actually beaten in Missouri, Montana, and Washington in the same election in which Eisenhower carried their states with majorities which ranged upward from fifty-one to fifty-nine per cent. of the total vote. In Indiana, conservative Senator Jenner was re-elected with a majority of only 110,000, but "Ike" carried the state by 335,000. In Wisconsin, Senator McCarthy was sent back to Washington with a 140,000 majority, getting fifty-four per cent. of the vote, but "Ike" got over sixty-one per cent. of the same vote and had a majority of 357,000. Even in Utah, conservative Senator Watkins had less than half the majority which "Ike" received in that sober-minded Mountain State.

The story on the progressive side of the Republican ledger is equally clear. Only one prominent "Ike-liker," Cabot Lodge of Massachusetts, failed of re-election, losing to young John Kennedy by seventy thousand votes, while Eisenhower swept the Bay State by more than two hundred thousand votes. In this case, the Taft Republicans knifed Lodge, while Kennedy ran on a more liberal program. However, in New Jersey the veteran liberal Senator Alexander Smith ran close to "Ike," getting fifty-six per cent. of the total vote while Eisenhower got a bit better than fifty-seven per cent. of the same electorate. And in New York State, the progressive Republican Senator Irving M. Ives almost equalled the Eisenhower vote. Ives actually received a plurality of 1,332,000 votes over his Democratic rival, as compared to "Ike's" 848,000 margin, but was helped by the attitude of the New York Liberal Party, a wholly-owned subsidiary of David Dubinsky's International Ladies Garment Workers Union, which supported Stevenson for President but cast 489,000 votes for a separate spite candidate for the senatorship.

So if the Republican Party is to succeed and hold office, it must obviously follow the "middle way" in politics, as developed by Dewey at Albany and represented in Washington by Irving Ives.

As with Dewey, Ives never wanted to enter politics in the first place and has been repeatedly trying to get out of politics ever since. He resents them but they fascinate him. Again like Dewey, every time he tries to return to private life, he goes up higher. On form alone his Senate colleagues expect to see him forced to run for (and be elected as) Governor of New York State whenever Dewey decides to evacuate Albany.

Irving Ives is another of these small-town, middle-class, old-stock Americans who illumine the Eisenhower movement like the stars in the flag. He was born and raised in the little town of Bainbridge, New York, not far from Oneonta, in a community of some thirteen hundred people, where everyone knows everybody else and where it still isn't necessary to lock your doors at night. His education was entirely normal for the community: first the public school, then Oneonta High School, and finally Hamilton College at Clinton, New York, which he entered in 1914.

His college education was interrupted, first by a serious illness and then by a serious war. He enlisted in the infantry, took instruction under a regular army captain named Eisenhower, and went overseas with the A.E.F., taking part in the St. Mihiel action and the bloody Meuse-Argonne offensive. On his discharge, he returned to Hamilton and graduated with the highest scholastic honors in 1920 at the age of twenty-four. He next got a job with the Guaranty Trust Company of New York and three years later went to Norwich, New York to handle upstate business for the Manufacturers Trust Company. Much to his surprise, he was elected to the New York State Assembly from Norwich after a squabble in the local Republican organization, and so gave up banking and went into that mainstay of the politician without a law degree, the insurance business. During thirteen consecutive terms in Albany, he became successively minority leader, speaker of the assembly, and Republican majority leader. He pioneered in labor legislation and achieved national prominence in 1945 for his part in framing the famous New York State Anti-Discrimination Law, the first legislation of its kind in America, which prohibits discrimination in employment because of race, creed, color, national origin, or ancestry.

Ives was also the author and sponsor of the state law which created the New York State School of Industrial and Labor Relations at Cornell University, and then resigned to become its first dean. Politics soon caught up with him again, and in 1946 he was nominated for the United States Senate and, thanks to Dewey's successful campaign for the governorship, won a smashing victory over the supposedly "unbeatable" former Governor Herbert Lehman. The landslide proportions of his re-election victory in the 1952 campaign automatically move him up to the king row of Republican candidates to succeed Tom Dewey at Albany.

Ives is of old New England ancestry originating in Connecticut, and traces his transatlantic descent back to the Norman Conquest when the original Yves came to England with William the Conqueror. He is a powerfully built man, with a strong voice, who delivers his addresses with force and conviction, while his record on labor, social, and related legislation is so outstandingly progressive that Colonel McCormick of the Chicago *Tribune* marked him down for reprisal and defeat in the 1952 campaign—which didn't hurt Ives at all in New York State.

His career, record, and character point clearly to the direction the New Republicans must follow if they wish to hold their majorities in Congress and develop progressive programs and policies under the Eisenhower administration. That is what the election returns declare and, so long as "Vox populi, vox dei" is a principle of representative government, the election returns are always right.

X

RENDEZVOUS WITH HISTORY

1. Unfinished Business

TWENTY years ago, Roosevelt and Hitler came to power almost simultaneously. Each had a mandate to restore prosperity and alleviate the social unrest caused by a great economic depression. Hitler soon took the road to rearmament and war, and Roosevelt followed his example, rather belatedly and in the face of deep national reluctance to be involved in another European conflict. The final test of strength between the American nation and the Third Reich, which resulted in the utter defeat of the axis, forced Roosevelt to abandon the measures—good and bad—adopted under his New Deal mandate of 1932 and 1936. But the problems with which those measures assumed to deal with remain the unfinished business of the United States.

Today, by a curious parallel, there has been a change in the governments of the United States and the Soviet Union as dramatic and as unpredictable as the earlier change which brought Roosevelt and Hitler to power in 1933. Stalin has died and his harsh Communist dictatorship over the Soviet empire and its satellites has been replaced by a new group under the comparatively unknown Malenkov. The change of régime in Moscow and Washington is one of the portents of our age. For the first time in many years the American people are represented by a strong President and a competent political administration. Roosevelt was a powerful political leader but an indifferent administrator. Truman was neither strong nor competent in his choice of administrators. Eisenhower and the New Republicans are powerful personalities and able executives.

Their basic duty in the worldwide conflict which has developed between the Soviet empire and the free world is to make and keep this country strong, free, and prosperous. Their domestic policy must, therefore, take precedence over all developments in our foreign policy short of war. They face a formidable task.

We have still to solve the problem of how to maintain a powerful military establishment without crippling taxes and without wasting the blood, toil, and treasure of our citizens.

We have still to bring our finances into balance, check inflation, and avert economic depression. The munitions economy inherited from the previous administration has provided employment and profit for millions of Americans; its replacement by an economy of production, distribution, and exchange will be difficult and may prove unpopular.

We must still solve the problem of employment, outside of defense and war production, in the face of the ever-growing industrial technology and the mechanization of production. The economic utilization of atomic energy alone will strike the roots of much employment in coal mining, railway transportation, and oil refining.

We have still to solve the problem of agricultural overproduction and of food prices which will be fair to both the farmers and considerate of the great majority of our citizens who do not live on farms and don't know one end of a cow from the udder.

We have still to strike the balance between social security and socialism, between individual initiative and collective responsibility, in meeting the hazards of old age, illness, and unemployment.

We have still to solve the problems imposed by the development of our great natural resources, especially those represented by water power, whether on the St. Lawrence River or in the Columbia River basin.

We have still to establish the appropriate role of private business, large or small, in the production and distribution of wealth, since the old evils of monopoly have inevitably returned as the end result of successful business competition.

We have still to devise the proper means by which a free people can defend their liberties from Communist conspiracy and still avoid the "deadly" peril of the police state.

We have still to establish the kind of steadfast foreign policy which will command the united support of our own people, the trust of our friends, and the respect of our enemies.

We also have still to discover the kind of foreign economic relationship with the rest of the world which will utilize our abundant production for the mutual advantage of ourselves and other nations, without running the risks of economic imperialism or incurring the liabilities of colonial exploitation of underdeveloped countries.

This is the unfinished business before the American people. To handle it successfully will be to lay the foundation for an impregnable defense. If we can show by our example that Moscow's dire predictions of capitalistic doom are mere Communistic wishful thinking, then we can deal resolutely with the larger challenge of Soviet aggression in the free world.

2. CHARACTER VS. COMMUNISM

The New Republicans represent the best we are so far capable of producing. The reserves on which the Eisenhower administration can draw are those of American character rather than national wealth. Only through men who represent a high standard of moral decency and broad humanity can we make an effective answer to the past suspicion and cruel fanaticism of the Communist conspirators. They are called upon to meet the challenge of this age.

The twentieth century is a tremendous period of revolutions, of liberation, and of mass destruction. Western science has released forces which could bring liberation to mankind, yet threaten us all with complete disaster. The world wars of this century have obscured the two great political events to which they gave birth: the Communist revolution in Russia and in China and the liberation of Asia, as a whole, from western rule.

America's power to survive the forces we have helped create will depend on the skill, strength, and determination we bring to bear on these twin developments which are now united in the form of an alliance between Soviet Russia and Soviet China.

America, as Eisenhower took control of its political government, stood at a height of prosperity and power. Our scientific achievements were stupendous. Our living standards and wealth were the highest in history. Having determined the outcome of the two world wars, we had achieved a position of decisive power in world affairs. We were challenged only by the Soviet empire, with its Marxist doctrine and its authoritarian state, and this challenge found us frightened and uneasy and increasingly uncertain as to the course we should follow.

Our science will not save us. The Soviet countries have science, too, and possess the resources to develop it independent of our pleasure. Our wealth will not save us.

History monotonously recites the tale of rich and prosperous countries which fell in the twinkling of an eye under the determined attack of hard, hungry, "inferior" peoples. Neither our standard of living nor the enormous physical resources of this continent can guarantee our safety or insure our survival any more than their beaten gold and jewels could save the Incas or the Aztecs from the Spaniards.

We cannot even count on maintaining our present position of relative power. At least twice in the history of the West a great power has emerged briefly, held the balance for a few years, and then dropped back into insignificance. In the fifth century before Christ, the rich city-state of Syracuse was swept into the great world war between Athens and Sparta. Syracuse turned the tide against Athens, but lacked the wisdom to bring peace to a Greek civilization which was destroying itself. Not rich and powerful Syracuse but obscure, semi-barbarous Macedonia was the ultimate victor in that contest. Again in 800 A.D. the Pope crowned Charlemagne as Roman Emperor. The great Frankish Empire stretched from the Pyrenees to the heart of Germany, from the English Channel to the Danube, and challenged the power of Byzantium. Yet after Charlemagne's death his empire fell to pieces, and not for another eight hundred years did France reappear as a great power in the world.

The great question is whether we, too, are under a doom.

The slow beat of observable climatic changes decrees that, for at least the next two or three centuries, the more northerly lands, Russia and Canada, shall become richer and mightier. Unless with our atomic mischief we should succeed in exploding this planet like a firecracker, there is nothing we can do to ward off the portent of a change as great as that which once drove the Northmen south to ravage Europe and colonize the Mediterranean world. The whole earth tends to become warmer as the polar ice-caps recede. We must begin to seek ways to adapt ourselves to this coming shift or it will destroy us.

The Eisenhower administration is mercifully relieved of responsibility for dealing with these predictable changes in the conditions of human life on this planet. It must deal with what is here and now; the most which can be expected of it is that it shall measure up to history and, so far as possible, place the people of this continent on the sunny side of future events.

Failure to deal wisely with the Communist revolutions in Russia and China and with the liberation of Asia has already brought us close to catastrophe. The cost of future failure could be extinction within a few short years. The cost of partial preparedness against the contingency of a third World War is already becoming prohibitive. The Defense Department estimates that it would require twenty billion dollars for aircraft and radar, and another seven billion for simple civil-defense arrangements, to achieve even moderately adequate security against transpolar atom bombers in the next two years. Even more costly would be the only fundamental defense against atomic bombs: to disperse our industries and break up our large cities so as to offer no major targets to the enemy. Biological defense would require still other and most costly measures. Political defense would require elaborate police arrangements which could destroy the traditional freedom we seek to defend. And in all these matters, the human element guarantees that there can be no complete security. Somebody can always slip, sleep, or betray his trust.

The defense of this country cannot, in fact, be assured by weapons alone or by the power of swift and terrible retaliation against attack. It must be political defense, an adjustment of ideas and interests which will render world peace as necessary as world war is catastrophic.

The first task of the New Republicans is, therefore, to understand the character of the Russian leaders, to realize how they became what they are and why they act as they do. The second task is to appreciate the long-smoldering resentment of the colored races of the world, in Africa and South America as well as in liberated Asia, against the manners as well as against the rule of the white nations who have governed the planet for the last two hundred years.

Here it is clear that the Eisenhower administration is far better equipped than was its predecessor to deal with the politics of peace and of racial readjustment. Not in this century has a Republican President brought this country into war. The Republicans have a genius for peace and commerce. They contrived the liberation of Cuba and prepared the independence of the Philippines as national goals, even while our troops were still fighting native insurrections. They negotiated peace between Russia and Japan in 1905. They made peace with Germany in 1921 and headed off the threat of a Pacific War in 1922. They are chiefly responsible for the recent peace of reconciliation with Japan. It is a fact that every single Democratic President in the twentieth century has involved this country in a serious war: Wilson in 1917, Roosevelt in 1941, Truman in 1950. It is unfair to hold the Democratic Party uniquely responsible for this national record, but the record itself stands as an indictment of the failure of Democratic diplomacy to avert or avoid the conflicts into which they led the nation.

On the issue of the colored races, the Republicans are also better able to speak to an Asia which is still hysterical and disorderly after liberation from white colonial empire. The Eisenhower Republicans are, personally and biologically, remarkably like the generation of men who fought our bitter four-year Civil War for the purpose of putting an end to Negro slavery in this country: deeply religious, old-stock Americans who did not shrink from the ordeal by fire. As in all wars, the motives of that conflict between the North and South were mixed, sordid as well as noble, but it remains true that the party of Abraham Lincoln and *The Battle Hymn of the Republic* did lead a great crusade to "die to make men free." It is also true that the southern Democrats, who still must live with the social and economic consequences of African slavery, tend to color and control the foreign policy of any Democratic President who might wish to deal intelligently with the ungainly, turbulent nationalism of the colored races of Asia which have recently regained their sovereignty from white rulers. The Republicans are relatively free from this crippling race prejudice.

These historical facts are among the resources on which Eisenhower can draw in his approach to the worldwide and almost irreconcilable conflict between the two great systems of thought, culture, and political power which stand embattled in this postwar era.

3. AMERICA OR RUSSIA

For thirty-five years, nearly two human generations, Russia has been ruled by a small group of despotic leaders: Lenin, Stalin, and now Malenkov, with their Communist party organization, their propaganda, their prisons, and their secret police. These men are absolutely committed, by their own writings and utterances, to the conquest of the world. They have dealt in lies and deceit, to their own people and to other nations, for so many years that it would be fatuous to accept in good faith any official Soviet assurance of a change of heart or abandonment of their established policies.

It would also be cruelly shortsighted to refuse to accept the possibility of such a change. Just as Roosevelt and Hitler represented the forces which combined to make the second World War, so it is conceivable that Eisenhower and Malenkov, between them, could restrain the ugly impulses which portend a third world conflict which would be the crowning catastrophe of white civilization.

The Eisenhower administration does not propose to relax our guard; it calls for deeds rather than words, and it contemplates a period of from ten to thirty years as the necessary condition for rebuilding good faith, if, indeed, war can be prevented. Yet in past Russian history there have been abrupt changes of policy with a sudden change of rulers. Even after thirty years of Stalin, there are forces in Russia which could support such a change.

Russia is still a part, although an heretical part, of that white western Christian civilization to which we, too, belong. Russian literature, Russian religion, Russian art and music, Russian science and industry, come from the West and not from Asia. Russia is, historically, the agent by which the religion and civilization of the West have been spread through Central Asia and to much of the Far East. Russia has been and can again become a creative spiritual force.

Marxist Communism has been perverted by the Soviet leaders into a doctrine of cynical absolutism. Even before his death Karl Marx denounced "Marxism." He was a German Jew who studied in England and combined in *Das Kapital* the moral denunciation proper to one of the Hebrew prophets with the intellectual apparatus of western philosophy. Thus, his now outdated doctrine has a common ancestry with the faith of the western world and, like that faith, bases itself on the great western concept of the brotherhood of man. Nothing that has come out of Asia since Buddha can parallel this concept. The Hindus devised a caste system which makes the Jim Crow policies of certain parts of this country look amateurish. The Chinese set up a cult of family devotion which excluded the ideal of love for one's neighbor. The original Marxist doctrine is not our enemy; it is only a tool in the hands of ruthless men, and a return to its first principles would render it harmless to humanity.

Since 1911 China has been exploding in revolution under the combined impact of Christian missions, Communist propaganda, and western technology. The upheaval which has begun in China and is beginning to shake India is an irreversible process. The great future problem before both Russia and America is to make sure that the terrible new powers which western science and teaching have introduced into Asia are controlled by ethical and moral standards which will prevent their abuse. Up to now the Kremlin has preached still more debased ethical concepts than those which Communism has displaced in China. This could be a doom for the entire world and must, out of the need for self-preservation, be stopp 1 until the Chinese have emerged from the dark ages of s perstition, cruelty, and tyranny which have been tradi .ional in Asia for thousands of years. The atom bomb or the plague bacillus in the hands of moral illiterates and political barbarians is nothing that either Moscow or Washington dares to contemplate.

That is why, high on the agenda of the deeds which the Soviet rulers must perform if good faith is ever to be restored, is the withdrawal of the false Communist charge of germ warfare against the United Nations forces in Korea. This lie must be thoroughly investigated, exposed, and denounced lest the millions of Asians whom it has deliberately deceived should conclude that future biological warfare is justified against the free world.

Other Soviet deeds swiftly suggest themselves: the negotiation of an Austrian peace treaty, the restoration of freedom to Czechoslovakia and Poland, the liberation of Germany, disarmament, control of atomic energy, the end of Communist intrigue in free Asia and throughout Africa and South America. These all represent actions by the Soviet state, its puppets and its agencies, which could accompany and justify the gradual release of tension between East and West.

There is one final test of Soviet sincerity and the professed will for peace on the part of the new régime in the Kremlin: the opening of political frontiers to travel and exchange of goods and the opening of human minds to discussion, comparison, and exchange of ideas. If the

Kremlin permits citizens of the free world to travel as easily within the Iron Curtain countries as Soviet subjects have been free to travel in the West, if Soviet citizens are free to read and believe and talk as they please, then the irrepressible conflict between America and Russia will be fought out on the level where it must eventually be decided: individual freedom to judge and choose. Granted such freedom, with rising Soviet living standards and twenty years of peace, the New Republicans may lead the whole world to peace after fifty years of universal tragedy and suffering.

If not, a war between Russia and America will be inevitable. If it comes it will be neither short nor pleasant. It would be the final downfall of white western civilization, since it would devastate if not destroy the two great protagonists of the intellectual and material forces that have at last created the prospect of a better and more secure life for the human race, as well as for its swift obliteration if they are mismanaged.

The only great power which would survive such a war would be China itself, since the Chinese still possess too decentralized a civilization to be vulnerable to atomic attack. Hence, the survivors of a Third World War might find that they had fought to make China the ruler of what remained of the world. Nothing in Chinese history, ancient or modern, encourages a belief that their rule would be preferable to a peace of reconciliation between America and Russia.

The task is not an easy one and does not rest entirely with the Eisenhower administration. It takes two to make a peace but only one to start a war. Yet this is the final test by which Eisenhower and the New Republicans will be judged by history, if there is anyone left to write history after the weapons of modern war have again been released upon the planet. The price of peace is always high, because it involves the pride and passions of men as well as their material interests. But today we have at least one more—and perhaps the last—chance to use our power and our wisdom and our character to bridge the gulf of suspicion, fear, and hatred which sunders the tragic, gifted, long-suffering people of Russia from the brotherhood of the free world.

INDEX

283